Social Media Marketing & Content Marketing for 2020

Growth Strategies to Stay Ahead in the Changing World of Digital Marketing and Maximize ROI.

I0510301

Authors:

Jaimason Bixley and Ralf Percy

Table of Contents

BOOK 1: SOCIAL MEDIA MARKETING 2019; THE ULTIMATE GUIDE TO BOOSTING YOUR BUSINESS THROUGH SOCIAL MEDIA MARKETING EFFORTS 1

INTRODUCTION 3

The Constantly Changing World of Social Media 3

The Magic of Social Media Marketing In Business 6

CHAPTER 1 9

Social Media Marketing - The Art of It... 9

Marketing Your Business on Facebook 9

Marketing Your Business on YouTube..................................... 12

Marketing your business on Instagram 14

CHAPTER 2 16

Developing a Working Social Media Marketing Strategy 16

Auditing Your Online Presence on Social Media Channels 17

Know Your Customers' Tastes and Preferences 19

A Mission Statement That Defines Your Brand............................ 22

Ascertain Key Success Metrics for Your Business......................... 23

CHAPTER 3 27

Social Media Monitoring and Listening.................................... 27

Understanding Social Media Listening.................................... 28

Understanding Social Media Monitoring.................................. 29

Tools To Make Social Monitoring and Listening Easier 30

Social Media Monitoring And Listening: Why It Matters? 31

CHAPTER 4 34

Developing a Content Strategy for Social Media Marketing 34
  Content Marketing Strategy and Its Importance 34

Choosing the Right Social Media Channel That Suits Your Brand ... 42
  Choosing the right platform 42
  Knowing your target audience 43
  What is your objective on social media? 43
  Audience behavior 44
  Having a balanced social media diet 44

Finding Your Brand's Voice on Social Media 45
  Work on reinforcing your brand's beliefs 45
  Carefully select the brand's voice 46
  Utilize a social customer service approach 47
  Consistent jargon 47
  Avoid bait and switch marketing technique 47
  Observe your audience engagement practices 48
  Taking pride in your brand 48

CHAPTER 5 50

Extending Your Social Media Reach 50

Focus your marketing efforts on the right target market 50
  Just Ask 51
  Number of Shares 51
  Watch Your Competitors 51
  Optimize Your Profile 52
  Share Evergreen Content 52
  Work smart 53
  Post on non-peak hours 53

The Right Content Matters Most 54

Marketing Your Social Profile Everywhere..55

Engaging With Your Followers for Successful Marketing 56

CHAPTER 6 57

Social Media Marketing - Building One on One Relations 57

Proof of care *58*

Regular communication...*58*

Host events *59*

Reward your Customers *59*

Consistency is key *59*

Increasing Customer Interest in Your Brand 60

Get Visual..*60*

Be Conversational..*61*

Get the right blend of engagement and action.......................................*61*

Make the best of social influencers..*61*

Give freely to get freely *62*

Personalizing the Social Media Experience 62

Collect adequate data *63*

Create customer personas *64*

Craft out your personalized content *64*

Personalizing the entire experience...*64*

CHAPTER 7 65

Fundamentals for Continued Success with Social Media Marketing 65

Sending the message of constant improvement..*66*

Growing your customer base..*66*

Taking advantage of multiple options *67*

Securing your company's future *67*

Social Media Channel Mix and Tactics...68

Create an Ideal Social Media Marketing Mix...................................69

Researching On Existing Competition 72

Broaden your search *73*

Rely on reports... *73*

Make use of social networks... *73*

Rely on your customers *74*

Ask your suppliers *74*

FINAL THOUGHTS **76**

BOOK 2: CONTENT MARKETING: GROWTH STRATEGIES TO STAY AHEAD IN THE CHANGING WORLD OF CONTENT MARKETING AND MAXIMIZE ROI.....................................**80**

BOOK SUMMARY: **80**

INTRODUCTION **82**

CHAPTER 1 BUILD AN OPT-IN OFFER.....................**84**

Here are some asset types for compelling opt-in offers: *85*

Build an Onboarding Sequence 86

Make Sales Offers.. 90

CHAPTER 2 THE MONEY IS IN THE FOLLOW-UP **94**

The Proactive Dashboard 101

Key takeaway: What can you stop doing today that isn't generating results?...103

CHAPTER 3 CREATING THE RIGHT CONTENT **107**

Define Your 10x Workflows 110

Determine When Each Task Should Be Done.................................... *115*

Estimate How Long Each Task Should Take...................................... *116*

Analyzing Content 120

How to Create the Best Content on Any Topic on the Internet............ *121*

Let's look at each step to put it to work in your 10x content. 126

Step One: Keyword Research *126*

Step Two: Analyze What's Ranking Now....................................... *127*

Step Three: 10x the Competition in the Face.......................................*128*

How to Use a Content Scorecard *132*

CHAPTER 4 WHO ARE YOU WRITING FOR? 137

Why is the Strategy Behind Free Content So Important? 138

CHAPTER 5 THE PROFILE OF A COPYWRITER.......................140

To have a little bit of talent *140*

You love to write...*140*

Be willing to start at low prices...*141*

Be confident about being different *141*

Be prepared to sell yourself *142*

Be prepared to become a Nazi grammar *142*

Develop Patience...*142*

A desire to speak up, with objectivity and humility *142*

Strategy and creativity *143*

Be available to write samples...*143*

Be open to new opportunities...*143*

Write/change a piece of content into a functional one; *144*

Sell a product/service *144*

Persuade the consumer...*144*

Use different styles of writing...*144*

Create Solutions 145

Style Formatting 147

The font...*147*

Use short paragraphs *148*

Word Play...*148*

Break the Rules *148*

Acceptability...*149*

CHAPTER 6 CLIENTS WANT PROVEN RESULTS....................150

The Power of Landing Pages 152

CHAPTER 7 CONTENT MARKETING FOR FACEBOOK MARKETING 165

Facebook Content Marketing *165*
Liking *166*
Sharing *167*
Clicking on links *167*
Appeal to people's emotions *167*
Use your target user's language and way of speaking *168*
Use words popular on the internet *168*
Use the "post description" to catch attention *168*
Use the power of the red arrow in photos. *169*

CONCLUSION 170

BONUS MATERIAL: PASSIVE INCOME IDEAS FOR 2020; A STEP BY STEP GUIDE TO EASY PASSIVE INCOME IDEAS FOR 2020 AND BEYOND 174

INTRODUCTION 176
Why the Need for Passive Income? *177*

CHAPTER 1: DROPSHIPPING 180
How Does Drop Shipping Work? *180*
How to Find Suppliers to Work with *182*
Attributes of a Good Supplier *184*
How to Pick the Right Product for Dropshipping *185*
Advantages of Dropshipping *186*
Disadvantages of Dropshipping *187*

CHAPTER 2 AFFILIATE MARKETING 189
4 Steps to Become a Product Creator *190*
4 Ways to Make Money as an Affiliate Marketer *192*
Advantages of Affiliate Marketing *194*
Disadvantages of Affiliate Marketing *195*
Mistakes to Avoid as A New Affiliate Marketer *196*

CHAPTER 3 PASSIVE INCOME INVESTMENTS 198
What Are Passive Income Investments? *198*
11 Examples of Passive Income Investments *199*
Advantages *203*

Disadvantages...*204*

CHECK OUT OUR OTHER AMAZING TITLES: 206

1. Resolving Anxiety and Panic Attacks 206

A Guide to Overcoming Severe Anxiety, Controlling Panic Attacks and Reclaiming Your Life Again 206

2. Cognitive Behavioral Therapy 208

How CBT Can Be Used to Rewire Your Brain, Stop Anxiety, and Overcome Depression...208

3. Effective Guide On How to Sleep Well Everyday 210

The Easy Method For Better Sleep, Insomnia And Chronic Sleep Problems 210

Dangers of Sleep deprivation. 211

How Much Sleep Do I Really Need? 213

Understand what Kind of a Sleeper Are You?.................................. 215

1. Lively, healthy early risers!...*216*
2. Relaxed and retired seniors..*216*
3. Dozing drones...*216*
4. Galley slaves...*216*
5. Insomniacs...*217*
So, which of the five groups do you think you fit into?.....................*217*

Simple techniques of preparing for bed 220

A Few Lifestyle Suggestions to Make You Sleep Better....................222

Book 1: Social Media Marketing 2019; The Ultimate Guide to Boosting Your Business Through Social Media Marketing Efforts

Book Summary:

Are you an entrepreneur that wants to use social media marketing to get the word out about your business online? You need an overview of what's out there so that you don't misstep in 2019.

Social media changes every other day. It's hard enough running a business without having to wonder what to do on your social platforms constantly. Luckily, there are ways you can boil things down, and focus on key high-earning processes that make SMM lucrative.

In *Social Media Marketing 2019*, I get right to the heart of boosting your business through platforms like Facebook, YouTube and Instagram. I'll help you understand which metrics to measure, and show you how to put together a winning content strategy for more customers, more often!

In this step-by-step guide you'll find out:

How to use Facebook, YouTube and Instagram for super-powered marketing

- How to develop a working social media marketing strategy

- About the secret insights hidden in monitoring and listening online

- Which social channels to invest in, and which to run away from

- How to target the best customers and build real relationships

- What your competition is doing and how to outstrip them

With so much information out there, you need a guide that gives it to you straight. You'll come away with a plan and a set of strategies that will drastically boost your online business.

Invest in social media marketing to accelerate your business growth, income and reach. It's up to you to take this information and change your life. Start now!

Get the latest strategies on SMM with this practical guide.

Get the book, make those sales!

Introduction

The Constantly Changing World of Social Media

Just a few years ago, running a successful business did not demand an online presence. With the rise of the internet, entrepreneurs began debating among themselves whether or not they should have an online presence. As a matter of fact, it was something optional. Whether you wanted to turn to the internet or merely run an ordinary business, it was up to you. Back in the halcyon days, business owners had the notion that running an online store was too expensive and that their target market would not bother searching them over the internet.

Well, today, things have drastically changed. The public is more aware of the products and services that they need. They are more knowledgeable than ever before regarding what they need and what they don't. What's worse, they have fingertip information regarding the brands that they should go for. Customers are now even aware of existing brand competition in the market. Thanks to the internet, they can conveniently shop from their homes.

Do you remember word of mouth marketing? Back in the golden days, local stores could depend on word of mouth marketing as a way of getting information about their products and services to their potential market. This meant that they only needed to provide quality products accompanied by excellent customer care services. After this, they hoped that customers loved their products/services. Also, they were quite confident that through word of mouth, their customers would appreciate them in front of their neighbors. When customers were not happy, it was an unfortunate thing for these businesses. Nonetheless, they were lucky enough that the message was only contained within their local surroundings. In any case, the negativity was soon forgotten. After all, folks have short memories.

Fast-forward just a few years, and we notice that only a small number of businesses do not have an online presence. Interestingly, the same customers that were purported as naïve are out actively searching for reviews about everything. They searched for cars, restaurants, TVs, groceries, and thousands of other products. It does not stop there. Their search also entails what other people are saying about your brand.

But the question is: do you have any idea about what they are saying about you? In the world of the internet, there is nowhere to hide. Whether you have a business website or not, people would still talk about you. You will only be left wondering and hoping that they talk something positive about the product and services that you are offering them. As such, having an online presence is of great importance to the success of your business. Today, this is not just a requirement; it is a necessity. Without an online presence, you just won't survive.

I remember just recently I was out on a wild trip, and I had to visit different restaurants here and there, wining and dining. I took different types of coffee; some were bad while some were good. But, I never bothered since I was new in the vicinity. If the coffee was terrible, well, you only find a magazine to read while you kill time, right? On returning home, I visited one of the websites where you get to be advised on the best places to visit. I left behind several reviews regarding the restaurants that I had visited. Just like the coffee I was served, some of these reviews were good, whereas some were contemptuous. My point is, with an online presence, it does not matter where you are located or how big your business is. People will still talk about your business. The worst thing is that you cannot stop them.

The question is whether you want to be actively aware of what your customers are saying out there? Do you want to engage in damage control whenever you feel like they are trashing your business reputation? Do you want to defend yourself by offering solutions to problems identified by your customers? Do you want to take charge of your publicity and ensure that your business image is not soiled? If your answer is yes, then this book will guide you through the world of LinkedIn, Twitter, Facebook, Instagram, and several other social media websites that will guarantee you a boost in your business marketing efforts. Indeed, it is by communicating with your customers on a personal level that you would be in a position to stand the competition that is coming your way.

One thing that you ought to understand about social media is that it is not all about dealing with what people are saying about your business. Instead, it entails communicating with your esteemed customers, listening to them, educating them, and working together to build a community. Through this communication, your customers would be in a position to know your business from every angle. They would know about the products and services that you offer, your workers, your integrity, and the culture of your organization.

Social media has created an online community where businesses get to interact with consumers of their products. The important thing that customers look for is a personalized experience. They expect to be treated as individuals and not just customers to purchase products. Businesses should bear this in mind when promoting their brands on social media pages.

Today, entrepreneurs will argue that it takes social media to grow a successful business.

This book will dive in further to help you in understanding what it means by marketing over social media. You will get to understand the best ways of developing a working social media strategy. Moreover, you will garner why it is crucial not only to listen to your customers but also to monitor them. This is not all; there is a lot to take home from this book. The best part is that you will ultimately grow your business if you pay heed to the recommendations that this book will be leaving behind with regard to social media marketing.

The Magic of Social Media Marketing In Business

So, now you understand why it is important to have an online presence, right? What is the next thing that you should do? It is quite unfortunate that many businesses fail in spite of their social media presence. We all know these businesses. They can be found on Facebook, websites, Google, LinkedIn, Twitter, you name it.

Although they have active social media pages over the internet, their businesses are not thriving as they should. So, what is the problem? Well, unfortunately, the Magic of social media is not working in their favor.

This brings us to the question: what is this "magic" that our businesses require as we try to compete for social media presence?

The above question can be answered by taking the time to understand your business expectations. Take, for example, the idea of coming up with a commercial. To ensure that the commercial is a success, one needs to produce it. A producer would have to understand the best times that the ad should be aired and for how long. They would also have to gauge and settle for the best outlet for their advert.

But how is the "magic" attained? Simply stated, the people or the team that you bring together will help you in accomplishing your expectations (the magic). For instance, it can be as simple as hiring an expert to re-post news for you. Alternatively, it can also call for technical assistance from an experienced online marketer. For this magic to work, business owners should have a diversified mentality of ensuring that every marketing idea is incorporated into the system and that it is working.

The team that will guarantee that the magic of social media works for your business would include web developers, writers, and marketers.

Web developer

The importance of a web developer in your social media marketing campaign cannot be overemphasized. An expert in this field will help you in laying out your business in the best way possible. I often call them builders. A good example of understanding how this works is through the way in which we stress on hiring accredited contractors to build our homes. We cannot just settle for anyone. I mean, they determine how our homes will look amidst those of our neighbors. If you choose a rogue builder, then you run the risk of living in a home that would be unpleasant. Same is the case with your online presence.

Before running up and down creating all types of social media accounts for your business, you should mull over hiring a web developer. A developer will help you in creating a professional website that delivers a good image of the company that you are running. Furthermore, a developer will take you through the nitty-gritty matters of your website including hyperlinking, Search Engine Optimization, and data integration. These are some of the things that you might not be accustomed to. Therefore, it is essential to begin your social media presence campaign by hiring a web developer.

Writer

One thing that I have learnt about social media is that "content is key." This is the phrase that you will see each time you browse looking for social media marketing tips. Well, it is true –content is key. And therefore, this is the main reason why you need a writer. You need someone who can deliver your long message concisely. Without an experienced writer, the chances are that you won't deliver your message to your customers in the best way possible.

Marketer

Another thing, for the "magic" to work in your favor, you will need the services of a marketer. A marketer will help you in strategizing how best to deliver the message about your brand. Depending on the business goals that you have in mind, an experienced marketer will be there to get you a working plan. Besides, they will work to ensure that your business is innovative enough. Assuming that you hire the right marketer with excellent qualifications, it is highly likely that your company would be ahead of your rivals. This would be attained through creative media campaigns.

Therefore, being on social media does not necessarily mean that the "magic" of social media works for you. It is very easy to get stuck in the highly competitive online environment. As such, it is imperative that you understand what it takes to have a social media presence that works for you. Do not just create social media accounts and expect followers. It doesn't work that way- trust me!

Chapter 1

"Sharing is the essence of social media"

-Zoe Sugg

Social Media Marketing - The Art of It

The art of social media marketing revolves around the idea of approaching or communicating with customers on social media platforms such as Facebook, LinkedIn, and Instagram. Today, businesses have turned to social media networks as a great place to meet and interact with their audiences. With the increased social media usage, more and more firms are rushing in to find their places on social media. It is for this reason that you will come across numerous websites providing guides on how to enhance your business' social media presence. Generally, the art of social media marketing entails companies using social platforms such as Facebook to promote their brands. Depending on the social media network, marketing techniques and tactics would vary.

The following few lines provide a concise analysis of the basics of marketing brands over social networks such as Facebook, Instagram, and YouTube.

Marketing Your Business on Facebook

Facebook is one of the leading social media websites at the moment. Therefore, this makes it a valuable tool to sell your business in the online community. However, most companies fail while marketing their businesses over this platform. Here's why.

The mere fact that you have a running Facebook account for your business does not mean that you should post anything. NO! First, you have to do your homework. Marketing your business on Facebook should not resemble the marketing tactics that you use to sell your business over television or radio. Moreover, the marketing strategies that you use should differ from those that you use when marketing your brand over magazines. The first thing that an entrepreneur should understand is how Facebook operates. Undeniably, people consider Facebook as their ideal fun space. This is where they get to interact socially with their friends and relatives. This means that as a business, you need to interact with them on the same level. You should join the conversation that is going on around the community. A big mistake that most businesses make is selling aggressively over Facebook.

Imagine what people in a particular social group would say when they try to discuss something important that is affecting the community, and yet, you are there pitching your brand. Marketing on Facebook demands that a marketer should learn to differentiate when to use hard-selling strategies. This implies that tactics such as frequently posting about a brand should be avoided in certain conversations. The last thing that you need for your business is having people "unfollowing" you. This is a negative statement that shows that there is something wrong you are doing on Facebook.

Another important aspect of marketing your business on Facebook is that people crave to communicate in a friendly and more human tone. Honestly, we cannot deny the fact that we hate when companies reply to our queries through automated emails. It shows that these companies do not have time for us. Similarly, when communicating with customers on Facebook, they expect a human tone. Therefore, it is vital for a business owner to find the right voice that would communicate to customers out there.

Whenever I am browsing through my Facebook page, I often get peeved when I notice that the same ad that was running yesterday is still showing on my wall. Well, perhaps, this is the same feeling that thousands of customers have out there. As such, marketing on Facebook demands that one should post regularly. Unlike conventional media, social media is all about being up to date. This is what socialites expect from your Facebook business page.

It goes without saying that the greatest form of entertainment comes from watching videos and skimming through pictures over Facebook. Interestingly, thousands of people get caught up watching funny videos and end up wasting their time there. But, guess what? This is what it takes to lure customers to your Facebook business page. Good use of pictures and videos will undeniably get people to like and share your brand. Isn't this what you want? If yes, then you should make use of them to ensure that your audience is constantly entertained.

Probably you are wondering what kind of pictures you should post on your Facebook business page. I would say relevant photos. Say, you are selling clothing outfits. This implies that you should take advantage of the Facebook platform to post images of your new stock. Get your customers talking and sharing by posting these pictures all over your wall.

Your social media page will not be successful if you choose not to learn more about your clientele. Fortunately, you can easily make use of Facebook Insights. These are tools that aid you in better understanding the kind of people that continuously like the products and services you offer. Once you are well aware of the people you are dealing with, it would be easy to modify your posts to suit their needs and expectations. In the end, you would be sure that you are posting the most suitable material to individuals that would highly likely share your brand for the rest of the world to see and probably turn to it.

It never gets enough with Facebook. The funny thing that you should not forget is that it calls for your patience when marketing your brand through this platform. Building stable relationships is not easy. Take your time to engage sincerely with your customer base. Do your homework; research on what you think is best for your clients. This is what they expect from you. Remember, rival brands are doing it, so should you.

Marketing Your Business on YouTube

A newbie will deny the fact that promoting a business on YouTube could be a great way to grow a business. Well, it is highly likely that they would think about the hustle and bustle of recording videos and uploading them. One thing that they should realize is that visual content is more popular on YouTube as compared to other social media channels. Consequently, this makes it an essential marketing tool for your business.

The opportunities for businesses to exploit YouTube are always on the rise. It is because about 85% of online adults regularly visit YouTube. This makes it a great place to market your brand. But before that, there are essential aspects that any marketer promoting their brand on this platform should be aware of.

A key to succeeding on YouTube is optimization. One is required to optimize their videos for Google search as well as for clicks. Let me make this easy for you to understand. Marketing on YouTube requires that you make good use of keywords in your tags, description, and in your titles. Why? Obviously, YouTubers would want to find videos related to your brand with ease. To fulfill this requirement, it is imperative to optimize your videos.

One of the recommendations that I found from Google is that you should begin with keywords, and then this should be followed by branding. For instance, a user looking for a cooking show would use the keywords –"cooking show." This should then be followed by what they were looking, for e.g., "cake tutorial." The last thing should be the branding, e.g., "Kelly Brown." Knowing how to optimize your videos would make a massive difference in landing numerous clicks directed to your brand.

Marketers on YouTube often forget that description is also essential in winning over a vast customer base. So, after watching a good ad, you forget to entice your clients about other products that they might be interested in. Well, guess what? That is the end of the tunnel. People will simply click on other videos probably belonging to your rivals. The sad news is that if your opponents pitch their message better than you, you are bound to fail.

Consequently, think about the idea of including a call to action message. Tell your customers why they should watch another video before they leave. Entice them. Play with their minds and rest assured that you will have them glued to your YouTube page. Do not make assumptions that customers out there will follow you automatically. Trust me they won't. Give them information about how they can subscribe to your YouTube channel for the latest information regarding products and services that you offer. If your pitch is outstanding, rest assured that you will get numerous subscribers.

There is something important that I need to mention here. Often, I have received questions about the kind of videos that one should post. Undeniably, being creative is the key to enticing your clients. Therefore, it makes sense that you first mull over the type of videos that you would be posting. Here are some ideas that should help you.

Post tutorial videos. Your audience is always in search of how best to use your product. Therefore, an excellent trick to attract their attention would be to post videos demonstrating how specific tasks are performed or just how easy it is to use your product. Most successful online marketers will also recommend the idea of posting product demos. Let's be honest, you won't incur losses by merely using some products to shoot product demos for your customers.

People are often convinced to turn to your product when they come across customer testimonials. Therefore, a brilliant idea for convincing your target market about your product is by posting videos featuring testimonials from satisfied clients. Also, you can opt to introduce your business through your YouTube channel. Introduce who you are as a business and mention the products and services that you offer. Remember, don't forget about optimization. It will make an immense difference in getting your audience to land in the right place.

Marketing your business on Instagram

With the growing number of Instagram users, this platform also presents itself as an ideal place to sell your business. There are more than 700 million monthly subscribers on Instagram. Therefore, this means that your product or service could quickly get a wide market reach. Unfortunately, this does not come on a silver platter.

Just like any other social media channel, Instagram is also a community. It infers that it is up to you to prove to the community that you are a valuable member of the platform. Constant participation is thus required from you. Just posting videos and images is not enough. Join the community. Be part of the conversation. Respond to questions from the community and make relevant comments. Without a doubt, this will get them talking and thinking about how valuable your brand is. Why? Because it is a part of the social community.

There are numerous ways of marketing your product or service on Instagram. Nevertheless, your message should not be confusing. Your brand should not be mistaken for another brand or something else. As such, consistency is critical. Assume you are marketing your product on Facebook using a different image. If you use a different image on Instagram, you run the risk of confusing your followers. They will never be sure about the actual product or service that you are selling. It is recommended that your brand's profile picture should be similar across all social platforms. Most importantly, it should be professional.

Instagram followers are always on the lookout for feeds that would interest them. Accordingly, your marketing efforts on this platform should include a reason as to why people should follow your brand. Make them aware of the difference that you would make if at all they chose to follow you. I always recommend a short and exciting bio that does not have a "salesy" tone.

Buyers in the modern world are frequently turned off by hard-selling habits. After posting images and videos about your brand, do not yell to your audience. The last thing that you should do is to pitch illusory sentiments about how your product is good. Give your audience time to make their comments without feeling that they are being pushed to the wall. Just be creative and not pushy.

Business owners should take their time to understand that their brands are out there to build a lasting relationship with their customers. Doing this right is, therefore, the key to succeeding in winning over customers. Once they are ready to shop, rest assured that they will come for your brand as you had already connected with them. So, focus on posting quality videos and pictures that will surely tempt your customers to keep sharing.

Chapter 2

Developing a Working Social Media Marketing Strategy

"The essence of strategy is choosing what not to do."

-Michael Porter

The easiest way to flop at marketing your business over social media is by rushing into it without having a solid plan or a working strategy. Sadly, this is what happens to most entrepreneurs and business owners. It could also happen to you. You can start a Facebook business page without knowing why you need it. What's worse is that you don't learn how you would measure if it is successful or not.

So, where should you start when developing a social media marketing strategy? This is the question that most business owners seek answers to.

The best place of beginning your social media marketing strategy is understanding the meaning of social media. You should get to know what it is and what it is not. Social media is not the run in the mill form of advertising or marketing. Social media entails the combination of technology with social interaction through sharing of images, videos, and words. In a nutshell, social media refers to "conversations" made convenient and richer.

Part of the strategy also includes listening to your customers, projections, and rivals in the same industry. Get to understand what your competitors are doing on social media. What are the customers saying about the products and services being offered? Is there a gap that needs to be filled?

Analyzing what customers are saying is an excellent way of getting to know them. The good news is that information can be attained by simply listening to conversations over social media. As a business owner, it would be your work to help your clients find answers to their queries. If possible rely on analytical tools which could range from basic tools such as Google Alerts to sophisticated tools such as Radian6.

Auditing Your Online Presence on Social Media Channels

Having understood the importance of a working plan when developing a social media marketing strategy, it is worth taking a look at the social media audit. Basically, this is a follow-up. What you are doing is that you are following up on the strategy that you are using to market your brand over social media.

What is a social media audit? It refers to the process whereby you take time to review what is working and what is not working in your strategy. Also, the process entails examining the areas that can be enhanced to guarantee the best results. It is quite likely that you think that the process would be challenging. Well, it isn't. Numerous social media analytic tools are at your disposal. With the help of these tools, the auditing process would be straightforward.

The main issue here is; how do you go about auditing your online presence on social media. A key step to take would be to review all social channels that your business is associated with. Take time to go through all the social channels without bias. Often, business owners would overlook other social channels since they are not popular. Whether you are running a popular social channel or a YouTube channel with only 20 subscribers, you have to consider them with equal importance.

Next, it is time to decide where you want to focus on depending on the product that you are dealing with. Here, most people would go for the top four social media channels such as Facebook, Twitter, LinkedIn, and Instagram. I cannot entirely say that focusing on a particular channel would not work. However, it is advisable to try as much as possible to invest in these channels equally. Bear in mind that their marketing returns would differ. Hence, it is never wise to put all your eggs in one basket.

Recording information is part of the social media auditing process. Here, you are required to record what you have found out regarding your analysis of the social channels that your business is linked with. Record the number of followers for each platform. Take note of the frequency of visits to the respective pages. How quickly do people respond to your posts over these platforms? Do you notice any changes with increasing posts from your end? These crucial facts will help you in gauging what works and what doesn't for your business.

As you scheme through your social media pages, it is essential that you check for consistency. Your brand should be represented in a way that it is not confusing to the audience. Consequently, if there is a website where you have slightly changed the logo, you should correct this with immediate effect. Ensure that you are keen on the colors that you use to guarantee consistency. Visitors accessing your videos on Instagram should have a similar perception when they access these videos on Facebook and LinkedIn.

Also, posts made on different social media sites should be compatible with the platforms in question. YouTube, for example, is a great place to post long videos. Shorter videos should be posted to other platforms such as Twitter, Facebook, or Instagram. Most importantly, unique content would appeal to your audience. For that reason, it is worth investing your money in creating innovative and engaging content for your audience to enjoy.

Social media auditing demands that you take the time to evaluate how your audience is interacting with the content you posted. One fact is that different social media pages will host various kinds of people. Take a look at Pinterest, for example. The platform has got more women as compared to men. In fact, over 70% of its users are women.

On the contrary, when you look at Google Plus, most users are men. So, before posting content over the different social pages, it is worth mulling over the content. Ask yourself if you are posting the right content to the right platform? A careful analysis of the content interaction with the market will aid in understanding your viewers better. Ultimately, you will end up posting relevant and engaging content which transforms into promising sales leads.

After auditing all your profiles for consistency and evaluating the content that you are posting, the next thing is to look forward. Decide on what is essential for your business growth over the coming few months. Set small yet achievable goals. One of your short-term goals could be increasing your followers or increasing the number of responses for a certain percentage. The results of your social media auditing should be saved for future reference.

Know Your Customers' Tastes and Preferences

Knowing your customers' tastes and preferences is key to any business success. This is because customers are the main determinants of the success of a business. After all, they are the source of business profits. Therefore, they are regarded as the most fundamental element of any business. Most companies that thrive in their market of operation often fulfill the promises that they make to their clients. However, meeting customer needs first requires that you understand them. It is imperative that a business owner should understand the customers to the extent that they can easily anticipate their needs and after that deliver beyond expectations.

Understanding customer tastes and preferences does not necessarily mean that one should engage with them on a personal level. Instead, it entails customer segmentation. Different customers would require different products and services. Therefore, a business owner could get to know his customers by coming up with focus groups. For example, if you are selling baby clothes, your target group would be mothers or rather parents having small kids. Developing focus groups requires that you segment your market based on gender, age, occupation, and disposable income. Doing this guarantees that you serve them better.

Customer shopping habits is another way of understanding them from a different perspective. What are some of the shopping trends that can be associated with your target market? Such shopping trends could be identified through the "Likes" and "Retweets" that your customers are posting or sharing. Certainly, if more customers like a specific product over social media, this means that they are looking to purchase it. Hence, a good move would be offering a discount coupon for that product over social media.

Similarly, shopping habits could be identified through customers' conversations. Often, people would want their friends to own products that work. Therefore, it is not surprising to find people frequently conversing that a particular brand is better than the other. This is where your business comes in. Understanding their tastes and preferences ensures that you are a step ahead of them. Before they know it, your social media page would be suggesting to them why your product suits their needs.

An important thing that companies should bear in mind is that they should find the best social media channel that suits them. Just because a rival brand is using Facebook to market its products does not mean that it would also work for you. You might end up making a terrible mistake by following the wind. Settling for an appropriate social channel is another way of getting to know your customers better. A business that deals with lady products would work best if it promotes its products over Pinterest as compared to Google Plus. It is because there are more women on Pinterest as compared to Google Plus. Hence, understanding your customers also demands that you choose the right channel to reach them.

Today, there are hundreds of brands in the market that are suffering as they failed to get personal with their customers. Getting to know your customers on a personal level is key to ensuring that your social media presence works to your advantage. When using social media to market products and services, business owners should understand that these platforms are there to bring them closer to their clients. Therefore, it is imperative to build long-lasting relationships with individuals over social media. Unfortunately, some businesses overlook this need. They ignore customer complaints posted on social media platforms. Some of them even send rude responses to clients forgetting that the success of the business depends on them. It is worth noting that minor issues can be escalated to the point of tarnishing a business' image. Consequently, companies are consistently advised to seek to build a personal relationship with their clients over social media pages that they are associated with.

Engaged customers on social media would defend a brand that they are loyal to. A business should consider these customers as their advocates. They are the individuals to convince other people regardless of the complaints that are being posted about your product or service. As such, it is good that businesses recognize this group of shoppers and reward them accordingly.

A marketing expert would not forget to mention the importance of constant engagement with customers over social media. Socialites are always out hunting for information. They want to be ahead of others in relation to products and services that they might be using. For that reason, work to give them what they need. Engage with them by continually informing them that there are new products set to be launched. Make your followers work as your brand ambassadors. If your pitch is excellent, you can expect good results.

A Mission Statement That Defines Your Brand

If you have been keen on the internet, you should have noticed that almost all businesses have mission statements. Why are these mission statements significant? In short, a mission statement is a statement that helps a company to remain focused on its goals. Your mission statement will, therefore, keep your head focused on the marketing goal that you have on social media.

Besides the social media strategy that you have in mind, having a mission statement is vital. Yes, you have all those goals on how you will increase your audience by a certain percentage or how you would boost your engagement. But you also need to have a target. An archer will never shoot blindly without having a goal to aim. The main idea here is that you need to have a sense of direction.

Don't fall into the trap where most business owners waste their time and money on social media just because it is a cheaper form of marketing. Cheap is expensive. You should have known that by know. Make use of social media as a marketing tool because you understand that it is an essential tool for achieving your business goals. So, a mission statement will act as a roadmap to guaranteeing that your social media use is a success.

Your mission statement should answer the specific results that you want or anticipate for your business now that you plan to use social media as a marketing tool. Also, an appropriate mission statement should detail where you will be focusing your efforts on the marketing campaign. And most of all, it should outline the primary reason as to why you opted to use social media as an ideal choice for your marketing demands.

Ascertain Key Success Metrics for Your Business

Once your business has its social media page up and running, there are other in-betweens that you should never forget to consider. The key success metrics that would help you in evaluating the success of your social media campaign are very crucial. Yes, you might be engaging with your customers, following them where possible, and rewarding your advocates accordingly. But, what is it you are doing to monitor and track the social interactions that you are indulging into? Measuring your activity on social media is a fundamental process in a successful social media marketing process. Through this analysis, it gives you an idea of what you are doing and whether it benefits your brand.

With the wide array of metrics that could help you in knowing your social media activity, it might prove a challenge when choosing the best. Some of the metrics that you could use include the volume of activity, reach, engagement, influence, and the rate of conversions. A key area in your marketing strategy would be to determine key success metrics that suit your brand best. Having a well laid out plan of the best metrics that you would be using would save you a lot of time. Moreover, it makes the process of understanding your brand's social presence to be relatively easy.

Volume, as a key success metric, helps in determining the overall impact of your brand on social media. Simply said, volume measures the number of people that are conversing about your brand. How many people are talking about the products and services that you offer? The perk of this metric is that it indicates interest among your audience. Hence, a large volume would mean that there is considerable interest in your brand.

Conversely, a small volume should not be taken negatively. After all, you want to know how your brand is performing out there. Therefore, a small volume should open your eyes to the fact that something needs to be done about your brand.

Maybe you are wondering how the volume of your brand can be increased. If this is the case, you don't have to worry as it only calls for extensive marketing efforts coupled with good content on your social media page. If your target market is not talking about your brand, then it means you need to hone your message. Find an experienced writer to do the work for you. Low volume could also indicate that your content does not appeal to your audience. Accordingly, you should move back to the drawing board and determine the kind of content your audience is after.

Without the right form of social media engagement with your audience, you can rest assured that you will not be winning your audience's trust anytime soon. Genuinely, "engagement" should be regarded as the most important metric for the success of your business. Just as the name suggests, engagement measures the way in which your audience interacts with your brand and the content you deliver them. What are the actions that your audience is taking on your posts? Do they like your content? Are they retweeting or sharing what you are posting? Are they commenting on your brand's attributes? These are some of the questions that the engagement metric will help you in answering. Measuring engagement demands that you pay attention to shares and likes, audience growth, mentions, and followers. Sharing engaging content is one of the recommended strategies for boosting your engagement level over social media.

Your ideal social media marketing strategy also entails deciding whether to amplify your message using "reach" metric. In comparison to the volume metric which measures the number of people conversing about your brand, reach metric measures the number of people that have gained access to your content. Thus, reach is a good indicator of the potential size of your audience. By utilizing this metric, one would be aware of the extent to which their content is shared across social media. In Facebook, for example, "total reach" will indicate the number of individuals that have seen your post.

On the bottom of this list, you will find influence as a metric. This is yet another metric that will help you understand the level of control you have over your target market. One fact you ought to understand here is that your audience size does not directly relate to influence. What does this mean? Just because an individual has a large number of followers does not mean that they can influence the followers to do anything. Your social influence on Facebook, Twitter, Instagram, and other social pages would be a useful metric in gauging your online presence.

Enhancing your social media influence is a long shot. It is a goal that is not easily attained. In fact, there are times when you will have to do the dirty work such as talking to yourself. Your audience should garner the feeling that they are on the same playing ground as you. Therefore, it is vital that a business owner engages with followers consistently. Following them and responding to their messages is something that you will have to do. There are no shortcuts to increasing your influence here.

Encouraging your followers to join the conversation and running contests and events are some of the ways of motivating your followers to engage directly with your brand. Considerably, you will also have to learn about how best to create content surrounding the most exciting topics and hashtags. By actively participating in social media through these strategies, there is no doubt that you would increase the chances of winning over clients to your page. Ultimately, influence, as a metric, aids a user in knowing how best to inspire action among their audiences.

Chapter 3

Social Media Monitoring and Listening

"Listening is a positive act: you have to put yourself out to do it."

-David Hockney

Social media monitoring and social listening are often used interchangeably. However, the two terms are entirely different as compared to what they mean. To make matters worse, numerous marketing software platforms use the terms to imply the same thing. I tend to differ with this. Social media monitoring refers to the way in which a user monitors conversations online regarding a particular brand, word, or phrase being used. On the other hand, social media listening is a practice whereby a user actively listens to and attempts to understand on-going online conversations about a certain brand, word, or phrase. Concerning the above definitions, these two terms should not be used synonymously as they mean two different things.

It could also be noted that social monitoring addresses customer issues on a micro scale. In this case, a business owner would respond to incoming issues, comments, and queries as part of engaging in social media monitoring. Here, a business owner monitors the on-going activity of a particular social media page such as Facebook.

Conversely, social listening tends to look at the activity of your social media accounts on a broader scale. The main focus is placed on how your audience talks about your brand. Data obtained from social monitoring comes handy here. This is because data from social media monitoring tells a lot about how customers are interacting with your brand and content over social media pages.

From the look of things, social media listening and social monitoring are somewhat confusing terms. Hence, the following few paragraphs would look at each concept independently for better understanding.

Understanding Social Media Listening

Just like other forms of conversations, listening is vital to the success of marketing over social media. Where do you start to listen? You might say that you should listen to your customers first. Well, I disagree. It is imperative that you begin by listening to yourself. Take time to listen to what you are telling your audience about the products and services that you offer them. What have you promised your audience regarding your brand? But most importantly, ask yourself which audience are you talking to? Which channels are you utilizing (Facebook, Twitter, or Instagram?) Are you using the right tone?

After that, listen to your target market over social media. What are they looking for? What are they saying about your brand? While doing this listening, you should not forget to listen to your rivals. Listening to them helps in evaluating the competition that is directed to your brand.

You must be wondering how best you can engage in social listening. Here's how. Find social mentions directed to your brand. While doing this, you should identify common terms associated with your brand. Maybe people are saying that your brand is the best. Others could be saying that your brand is out of this world. Social mentions will help you understand your clients and how they relate to your brand.

A recommended practice when engaging in social listening is to react. Don't just sit there and watch as your clients talk about your brand; you must react. Think of social media listening as a vehicle that you are driving to get to your most-esteemed clients. Yes, it is possible to use it to get to your last stop faster. However, you are the one to steer the wheel. Hence, the best way to listen is not just to listen but to also react. Respond to your mentions and make appropriate comments where necessary.

Active listening also requires that you establish the rush hours. Find out the most active times when your audience is engaged on social media. Doing this warrants that you are always on time to listen to them.

Your customers expect that you carefully listen to them. Never be quick to assume the issues and negative comments coming from your audience. Respond to them accordingly to develop a trustworthy brand in their eyes.

Understanding Social Media Monitoring

There are many factors to consider when practicing social media monitoring for your business. You could monitor conversations that mention your brand. After that, you should take the time to evaluate whether the activity pays off for your business. Social media monitoring would majorly revolve around the tools that would make the process easy. Nonetheless, a user should be careful to understand that they are monitoring conversations. It is the first step to knowing what is worth tracking.

A business owner monitoring their brand, for example, would be careful to observe things such as brand name misspellings, catchphrases, names of active members of the company, and perhaps the campaigns for the brand.

If you are out monitoring for topics that are closely related to your product, then you should be monitoring things such as keywords related to your brand. Phrases that possibly refer to your product and service could also be monitored. Similarly, you should not forget to monitor common hashtags that are used in the industry that you operate in.

Social media monitoring also entails knowing how to monitor. This means that you will have to learn from the best on how they monitor social activity. Tools are mostly used for successful social monitoring. There are a wide array of tools that would be discussed succinctly in the following few paragraphs. Just to mention a few of these tools, you have the freedom of using Google Alerts, Social Mention, and Talkwalker among other social monitoring tools. It is always advisable to choose the right tools recommended by experts out there. As such, it will save you a lot of money if you conducted extensive research on ideal tools to run.

Tools To Make Social Monitoring and Listening Easier

Tools are mostly used for social monitoring and listening. A keen review of these tools will reveal the fact that they operate in almost the same manner. Interestingly, certain software platforms would offer their product as a tool used for social listening and not for social monitoring. Regardless, these tools have proven to be handy in understanding how your business is faring over different social media platforms.

7 of the best common tools for social media monitoring include:

1. Keyhole

2. Twitter Counter

3. Hootsuite

4. Digimind

5. Klout

6. Zoho Social

7. Simply Measured

8. Buffer

Before settling on any of the social monitoring tools above, it is essential to find out the monitoring options that are available when using the tool. It is important to do this because different tools would allow monitoring on specific websites. Keyhole, for example, allows monitoring on Instagram and Twitter accounts. On the other hand, Hootsuite enables monitoring across a wide array of social networks including Facebook, Twitter, LinkedIn, Foursquare, and WordPress. Keeping this in mind, it is worthwhile that you do your homework on a monitoring tool that meets your needs.

4 of the best common tools for social listening include:

1. Mention

2. IFTTT

3. Hootsuite

4. Keyhole

Just as mentioned above, a user should dig in deeper to find out the social media platforms that are supported when using these tools. Please ensure that you do not end up settling for a monitoring or listening tool simply because of popularity. The best way of finding out whether you have chosen the right tool is by going through reviews featuring these tools. Indeed, you would get the info that you need to make the right decisions.

Social Media Monitoring And Listening: Why It Matters?

With all the information on social media monitoring and listening, it is worth questioning why this activity is of great importance to your business. One of the main benefits of social monitoring and listening is, of course, the gathering of information. Listening is undeniably a good way of enhancing your business. In line with monitoring, it involves the process of monitoring conversations that touch on your brand. However, today data is quite overloaded over the internet. It makes it even harder to find out everything about your brand. Luckily enough, there are monitoring tools that make it easy to know when one mentions your brand. Therefore, monitoring and listening tools help in gathering essential information about a particular brand.

Monitoring and listening on social media also ensure that consumer engagement is enhanced over time. How is this possible? When a business owner goes through their mentions over social media platforms, they discover ideal ways of dealing with their audience from a personal level. For example, business owners would have an opportunity of reacting to client's issues. This gives followers a positive image of the brand. Customers would gain the perception that the business truly cares about their needs and preferences. Eventually, consumer engagement is significantly improved over time.

The constant changes in the competitive business environment that we live in makes it challenging to adjust and counter competition. Luckily, technology has made it possible to find time to work on certain things such as product development. With the help of monitoring and listening tools, for example, business owners get extra time to design and implement improvements to their brands. In the end, a brand is continuously developed to match the needs and expectations of clients. All these would not have been possible without the help of social media monitoring and listening tools.

In essence, numerous benefits can be obtained through social media monitoring and listening. Nonetheless, the main advantages of social media monitoring and listening include:

- Gaining access to an unlimited number of conversations
- Comprehensive data analysis
- Prevents social media crises
- Enhancing client relationships
- Genuine feedback from the audience
- Realizing new sales prospects
- Effective control over online brand perception
- Learning and adapting to improvement trends

Chapter 4

"Your content has no value unless it moves, unless people see it, engage with it and actively share it."

-Mark Schaefer

Developing a Content Strategy for Social Media Marketing

Content Marketing Strategy and Its Importance

The rise of the internet has undeniably made competition for customers even stiffer. Businesses have been left in a dilemma as they no longer have time to ponder on how best to approach their consumers. Most companies have, therefore, turned to social media as the best option of marketing their products to their clients. It is a move that has proven to be successful as most businesses are already reaping its fruits. It should be kept in mind that the success of using social media to market products and services does not come overnight. It demands patience from the business owner as numerous things come into play.

Content is one of the most important things to consider when setting up your social media marketing campaign. Content will get people talking about you and your brand over social media. The content that you deliver to your audience will make a massive difference to your business. This is because it would determine whether or not you would achieve your social media objectives. For instance, say your social media objective is to enhance your brand recognition. Here, the content strategy that you adopt ought to specify the rate of posting on your Facebook business page. Other plans to directly engage with your consumers could also be mentioned. This gives you the advantage of exploiting the opportunities available in connecting with your prospects.

There are four critical elements of social media content strategy. These components are succinctly discussed below.

Research and Analysis

The easiest way to fail when marketing your brand on social media is failing to do your homework. You can't just wake up and assume that your audience will fall in love with anything that you would be posting. If you ask the professionals, it doesn't work that way. First, you have to engage in in-depth research. Research is key to understanding what works with your audience. Your social media audit would be handy in this case. It will help you gauge how your audience reacts to specific posts. Social media monitoring tools will also be of great importance in knowing the demographics of your audience. That way, you get to post relevant content to the right group of people.

Once you have done your research, next in line is to analyze the content that is suitable for your audience. Find out how your audience reacted to the previous posts. Take note of the posts that have been performing really well. This should give you a rough idea of what your audience expects. It is vital that you consider performing this analysis in all the social networks that your business is linked with. This is because your audience would vary depending on the social networks that they are subscribed to. Indeed, there are instances where you find that your Instagram page is performing well with posts on "how to."

Conversely, your Facebook page could perform well with inspirational posts. Therefore, it is imperative to do some analysis on the different networks and how your audience relates to posted content. Don't make assumptions or generalize your content.

Wait! Don't stop there. If possible, dig in deeper to talk to your audience on a more personal level. Some social media marketers would even recommend the idea of asking your audience what content they anticipate in the future. You can never go wrong if you choose to ask them. It could be a great idea of finding insights into content that is engaging.

Also, don't forget to work with your team of content creators. This includes the likes of marketers and copywriters. Inform them about the ideas that you have found out. Share with them to ensure that the social media marketing objectives do not collide on the way.

Competitive Analysis

You might have made a wild guess on what you should be doing here. With regard to content, your rivals can be a great source of inspiration. Hence, instead of being jealous of their performance, you can use them to gain inspiration on the right content that will entice your audience. What are they posting? If you are dealing with the same products, you might want to ask -which group of clients are they focusing on? The most vital question is of course whether they are making conversions.

Often, we have come across the phrase "learn from the best." Truly, the last thing that you should be doing is paying attention to competitors that are not in your league. Try to emulate the big players in the market. I mean, that is where you want to be, right? Thus, find out what they are doing, and you will fill up the gaps in your social media content strategy.

Goals

After doing some in-depth research and learning from your competitors, the next thing to do would be to set goals that suit your specific type of business. A big mistake that most business owners make is copying everything that they see their rivals do. Do this, and you will fail terribly. The goals that you will be setting here are content-performance goals. It is worth noting that your content goal should be related to your social media marketing objective. If your Facebook objective is to increase the reach, the parallel content goal would be to increase the number of shares over a certain period.

Distribution

Another essential component of your social media marketing strategy is distribution. What are the different types of content that you would be posting to various social networks? How often will you be making these posts? When deciding on what to post, you should refer back to your social media audit. Data obtained here will tell you what content goes where and how often. The content research that you previously did should also give you an insight into the right content that should be posted based on its previous performance. One crucial fact, however, is that content posted over varying pages could differ. Nevertheless, your brand voice should remain the same all through. Do not confuse your audience by using a different tone from one social media network to the other. Embrace consistency.

Developing Actionable Key Performance Indicators

After having understood the importance of developing a content strategy for your social media marketing campaign, the next thing you would be doing is measuring your performance. This is a crucial step as it ensures that you are on the right track with regard to marketing your brand over social networks. There is a valid reason as to why you are promoting your brand on social networks such as Facebook, LinkedIn, and YouTube. Maybe you are looking to find more followers for your brand. Perhaps you want to enhance your reach. Well, with all these objectives in mind, you definitely need to measure how well you are performing over these social networks.

When it comes to marketing on social media, one can never be confident that they are posting the right content or engaging in the right marketing campaign. Therefore, measuring your performance over social media is imperative. Results obtained will help in getting insights on how you can formulate or adjust your goals to meet your marketing objectives.

Most businesses, however, have the perception that measuring performance is just about tracking "retweets" and "likes." This is not true. Performance measurement goes beyond that, and it includes going through some key performance indicators (KPIs). Some of the most important KPIs that will aid in better understanding how well your campaigns are faring are discussed in the following paragraphs.

KPIs suited for Reach

Reach is a metric that tells you more about the number of people that have seen your message. Measuring reach is made easy through the use of the following key performance indicators:

Follower Count

In any scenario, the number of followers that one has is a likely indication that their content is reaching thousands of people. In the same manner, the number of people following a particular business over social media page is a good indication that their content is reaching many people. The number of followers does not automatically mean that all followers would influence your brand.

Nonetheless, it is still a good sign that your content is reaching out to as many people as you want. This is a good performance indicator that your content is working out. You only need to polish your content to ensure that you convert many followers into loyal customers.

Web Traffic

The amount of web traffic coming to your website from your social media connects, is a likely indication that your content is interesting. It tells a lot about how your audience is interacting with the content that you post over your social networks. Undeniably, if the content was not good, they would not bother visiting your business website. Business owners should take this to their advantage and try their best to convert their followers into customers.

Your Brand's Voice

Your brand's voice is a metric that will tell you a lot about the conversation that surrounds your product or service. It gives you an insight into what people are saying about your brand as compared to your rival brands. It goes without saying that if your brand lacks voice out there, then it means that your content is not appealing to your audience. This shows that it is time to pay attention to your rival brands and emulate their good strategies. Remember, it is advisable not to copy social media marketing strategies from your rivals. You need to learn from them and adjust accordingly.

KPIs Suited for Engagement

Online marketers will argue that this is perhaps the best metric to help you in measuring your performance over social media networks. Basically, it takes into consideration the number of comments, likes, and shares. What your engagement KPIs do is that they ensure you garner awareness on how active you are over social media pages such as Twitter and Facebook.

Common key performance indicators suited for engagement include:

Clicks

Clicks refer to the number of "clicks" that you are getting on your business social media page. The more clicks you have that lead your audience to your business page, the more likely you are to win them over. Clicks and traffic are two different things. You might get huge traffic, and yet no visitors are directed to your business website. Therefore, with a high number of clicks, there is a reason to smile as you are one step away from winning over customers to depend on your brand.

One important thing to keep in mind when measuring performance using clicks is that you should also mull over shares, bounce rate, and likes. You might have a good number of clicks accompanied by a high bounce rate. This is a red flag. It is an indication that your content is not appealing to your audience despite your effective social media marketing strategies. Thus, when this happens, you need to find an expert to help you work on your landing pages. A low number of shares is another red flag to be wary of. Evidently, if people are not sharing your content with their friends and relatives, then chances are that your brand is not selling. Find out why!

Shares

"Shares" is another KPI that will help you measure how best your content is selling your brand out there. What does it mean to have more shares on your social media page? Well, a good number of shares is a probable indication that your audience is willing to recommend whatever you are selling. We live in a time when everybody is out looking for social media proof. And so, having a high number of shares will help you a lot in increasing brand loyalty.

Likes

In comparison to shares, "likes" do not accurately indicate whether your content is performing well in different social media networks. Personally, there are times when I find myself hitting the "like" button on Facebook without taking into consideration the brand I am liking. Therefore, this KPI could be misleading at times. But, on the bright side, the number of likes on your brand could tell a lot about the attention you are generating amongst your audience.

Psychologically, people fancy the idea of associating themselves with things that are nice and worth turning to. Therefore, if we think from a positive angle, the high number of likes for your brand could indicate that your brand is good or that your content is nice. It is a good sign that you are doing a nice job in attracting attention to your brand. The next thing to do here is to simply find ways of engaging your audience.

Mentions

Just as the name suggests, mentions refer to the way in which a specific conversation goes around your brand. What are people saying about your product or service? Depending on your brand name, keywords, or phrases associated with your brand, people will mention you in their conversation. Knowing what they are saying is an essential measure of your performance. A positive talk surrounding your brand will undeniably mean that your content is selling your brand.

Comments

The purpose of social media is to communicate and engage with your audiences. These are individuals that want to get to know more about your brand. Similarly, comments could be about the simple things that are linked to your brand and could include issues that that community is going through. Therefore, when pitching your brand on social media, it is worth knowing when to stop talking about your brand. People expect you to listen to them and not just yell to them about how good your product is. An excellent way to pitch your brand would be to first get the conversation going about how people meet a certain need. After that, you can leave a tip behind informing your audience or chat group about the solution that you offer. See! First, get your audience to talk.

Choosing the Right Social Media Channel That Suits Your Brand

Facebook, Pinterest, Instagram, YouTube, or Twitter are the best platforms to invest in when it comes to business social media marketing, right? Well, you might be wrong if you thought that going for the best ranked social media pages would mean that your business would highly likely thrive. As a matter of fact, this is the worst mistake that most business owners make. They end up going for Facebook as their ideal platform to market their brand. Later on, they realize that their brand might have performed better if at all they marketed it over Twitter or Pinterest. What am I trying to say here? Depending on your brand, some social media platforms might work whereas others might not. So, do your research prior to settling for any.

Choosing the right platform

Research shows that there is no indication that the rate of social media growth is declining anytime soon. Therefore, this is good news to business owners as they still have a lot to cover to ensure that they fully exploit the world of social media. With the continued increase in the use of social media, it begs to question which social media pages are mostly used depending on geographical locations. One thing for sure is that social media is unevenly distributed throughout the entire world. Do you know that Facebook is not the most popular social media channel in China? If you don't, now you know! WeChat is a social media platform that is ranked as the best in China. If you go to Russia, you will find VKontakte is the best social media page to be associated with.

Perhaps you get the idea of where we are going. Choosing the right social media platform does not necessarily depend on the rankings that you have heard on numerous media channels. There are other things to take into consideration including geographical distribution. Other factors to put in mind are briefly discussed in the following sections.

Knowing your target audience

Before spending your resources on a social media platform that would not suit your brand, it is important to consider what you know about your target audience. First, who are they? What are they searching for? And on which social media platforms are they most active? What are they mostly doing on social media networks? What is their preferred choice of interaction over social media? These are some of the questions that you should be asking yourself about your target audience.

If your prospects are most active on Facebook, Twitter, or Instagram, it means that these are the social media pages that you should pay attention to. Remember to balance your equation and ensure that other pages are also considered in moderation.

What is your objective on social media?

Your social media marketing objectives will also have a huge influence on the platforms that you will be choosing. Are you planning to grow your reach? Are you seeking to enhance your engagement levels? Do you plan to increase your audience? The goals that you have in mind should match with the right platform that will guarantee you achieve your goals. For example, because you want to engage more with your audience, Facebook could be an excellent place to start. Additionally, if your goal is to boost traffic to your business webpage, then Instagram could be your ideal social media platform to invest heavily on.

Audience behavior

The ever-growing social media presence is perhaps influenced by individuals using more than one social network to communicate. Marketers should not overlook this behavior. What do we learn from how people use more than one social networks? With billions of people spread all through the different social networks, we can only argue that they have an array of desired outcomes and objectives. For instance, some people might rely on Facebook to keep in touch with their friend. On the other hand, some would opt to use YouTube to entertain themselves by accessing videos posted on the platform. As you can see, different demands influence people's social behavior over these platforms.

By understanding the varying audience behaviors as they access social media networks, marketers are better placed to formulate ideal social media marketing strategies. In this case, you will know exactly what to post where and why. An important fact to keep in mind though is that all across the different platforms, you will meet with similar people. So, it is imperative that you understand the best way of exploiting each social media platform.

Having a balanced social media diet

With the perfect understanding that you will find the same people that you found in some of the channels you are promoting your brand on, you should not share an exact message all through. This portrays you as dull. Your followers will quickly get bored with your posts. As such, there is a good chance that they would be overlooking them. Ensure that you balance the way you post content across all the social media channels that your business is associated with. Balanced and creative use of social media networks would highly likely increase your reach. Hopefully, if you play your cards right, you will increase the number of shares given time.

Finding Your Brand's Voice on Social Media

With the vast array of social media channels at your disposal, there is no doubt that your brand's voice might get lost along the way. Unfortunately, this is where most business owners fail. They invest in social media networks, but they fail to maintain consistency across the platforms.

What's worse is that consumers get confused with the similarity of the ads that are posted on social media. Two or more brands could run similar ads, and this could be confusing to the audience. Ultimately, you might end up losing your loyal customers to rival brands. So, how do you go around the idea of maintaining your brand's voice on social media to guarantee that you remain unique in the market?

Work on reinforcing your brand's beliefs

The belief that you have about your brand would form the perception that you would be creating in the minds of your prospects. What do you want them to perceive your company or business? Do you want them to think that you are a friendly company? Alternatively, you might want your audience to believe that you are a valuable company. All these ideas define your brand's beliefs.

Research tells us that consumers on social media pages are often after honesty from businesses. It is worth noting that most consumers dislike snarky attitudes from businesses. The point here is that it is worth understanding the tone that matches your business' beliefs. The tone that you are using to communicate to your audience over social media should run parallel to the beliefs that your business advocates for.

The advantage of maintaining and reinforcing your brand's beliefs in your communication attributes is that it creates some form of consistency. Hence, if a customer comes across a snarky attitude in your conversation, they would question themselves whether they are interacting with the right brand. Recognizable actions such as these define you. It helps you in creating a unique social identity among your audiences. Undeniably, it is one of the winning ways to distinguish yourself from the competition in the industry.

Carefully select the brand's voice

Maybe you are still confused about how you can find your right brand's voice on social media. One fact is that when your audience understands how you communicate, this means that your social media business marketing activity is made easier. Formulating posts and tweets would not be difficult.

Let's stop there for a moment and reflect on some of the main reasons why customers unfollow brands that they had initially been loyal to. One of the main reasons is, of course, being embarrassed. When consumers feel embarrassed with your posts, the last thing they want is to be associated with you or your brand. Automatically, you will be unfollowed. Secondly, customers might choose to unfollow a particular brand simply because the content posted is irrelevant. It does not suit them in any way.

The dilemma facing businesses is finding the right ways to keep their audiences entertained. Undeniably, this is a daunting task. You can never please everyone. If you try doing it, you will fail terribly.

With regard to your brand's voice, a clear voice ought to be maintained in every post and tweet that you make. Suggested tips that could help you maintain a clear voice include:

Utilize a social customer service approach

If you have been shopping over the internet, you must have come across hundreds of angry customers. It is a typical thing that happens to any business regardless of its position in the market. Thus, it is important to anticipate that you would be dealing with angry customers over social media. So, how best do you approach a situation where a customer lashes out words for a product or service that they did not like? Saying sorry is not enough. The customer expects more than just saying sorry. Here, an ideal strategy would be to have a similar goal that ensures customer complaints are adequately dealt with. Your strategy should also encompass the idea of having a team ready to interact with customers and find amicable solutions to their problems.

Consistent jargon

Your brand's identity would be influenced by the jargon that you choose to use on different social media pages. This also bears an impact on the quality of content that you would be posting. If you choose to use an expert on your Facebook posts, ensure that you do the same on Twitter. Don't give your audience time to think that two different people are running the same social media account. Consistency is what you are after.

Avoid bait and switch marketing technique

Now that you are trying to maintain a consistent brand voice, it is not wise to try out bait and switch selling technique. It is a technique where a brand advertises its products or services at a considerably low price. However, when a customer visits the website to purchase a product, they realize that the discounted product or service is not available.

Customers that have depended on your product or service more than once will feel as though they are being tricked. Therefore, there is a high possibility that trust issues would be raised if you employ this selling technique over social media channels.

Observe your audience engagement practices

Like I have said before, audience engagement sells your brand on social media. Posting status updates and commenting on customer queries is part of telling them who you are. It reveals to them how different your brand is. The point here is that the way you post and respond to your audience matters a lot with regard to maintaining your brand's voice. The tone you use to address customer issues should be similar all through the social platforms that your business is linked with. Doing this ensures that your customers never get confused while dealing with your brand. Remember, the perception that they have about your brand sticks on their minds. A good impression will, therefore, increase the number of shares.

A point to take home is that your engagement could be improved with the help of social-monitoring tools. These tech tools give you an easier time classifying messages that need a specific response. Thus, you would be working smarter while at the same time ensuring that your brand's identity sticks to the audience's minds. But to do this correctly, you need to monitor and listen to your messages carefully. This is the only way that you would create a lasting impression.

Taking pride in your brand

Standing out from the rest of the lot is a challenging task. Nevertheless, this does not mean that you should give up. Take pride in your brand

and understand that your consistent brand's voice will ultimately pay off. The good news is that when customers learn to recognize and differentiate you from others, social media engagement is a lot easier.

Chapter 5

Extending Your Social Media Reach

"Social media allows big companies to act small again."

-Jay Baer.

As I had described before, social media reach refers to the total number of individuals that gain access or see your content. Now that you understand what reach means, it is time to find out how you can increase your reach. Certainly, expanding your reach means that your social media content would be reaching to many prospects as compared to your initial social media marketing efforts.

This section dives in further to take a look at some of the ways in which you can increase your reach. Whether you have a small or large business, extending your reach is crucial as it guarantees you that your message is reaching many potential individuals out there. For a small business, understanding the tips and tricks of doing this saves you the burden of having to pay marketers to help you in marketing your business over social media networks.

Focus your marketing efforts on the right target market

Most companies out there would have the perception that they need to have an online presence on all social media pages including Facebook, Instagram, and Pinterest. Well, this is not true. One thing that you should consider is that not all audiences have Facebook accounts. Similarly, some of them might spend less time on Instagram. As such, businesses should understand that focusing their marketing efforts on the right audience increases their chances of succeeding.

So, how do you know the best platform that suits your audience?

Just Ask

There are several ways of knowing the right platform that works for you. Why don't you try asking your audience? To do this, you need to post surveys asking them about the social media platforms that they usually use. Record this in a table and classify them accordingly. With this information, you will surely know where to channel your marketing efforts. In the long run, you will not be wasting time trying out all social media networks.

Number of Shares

If you are running a company website, then you should be making use of share buttons on your page. With the help of this tool, you can get information regarding the number of shares that are made on your website. Moreover, you also get insights concerning who is sharing such information and to which other sites. From this, you can easily know the most popular social media pages where your audience is sharing information. After that, your work would be to invest in getting relevant content posted on popular social media pages among your followers.

Watch Your Competitors

You could also take advantage of the actions of your competitors regarding how they are sharing content over different social media pages. Where are your competitors in the same industry posting? If they are not posting on a particular platform, then this is not the right place for you to post. Find a common place where your competitors are busy sharing posts. This makes the process of identifying a good social media platform to be relatively easy. As such, you get to reap the benefits of posting content on a page that guarantees a high reach.

Optimize Your Profile

Something interesting about dealing with Google is that you will always have to optimize your content to ensure that you benefit from doing business over the internet. Well, it turns out that social media pages also work in the same manner. Your social media business profile should be optimized for better visibility.

Some proven tricks will help you in optimizing your business profile to guarantee it can be easily found. It is worth pointing out that there are times when customers would want to find your brand on social platforms. Therefore, your duty should be to make the process easier for them. Your rivals are doing this. They are doing their best to make sure that they can be found by just typing a particular keyword or phrase. Is this what you have been doing? If not, here are some good tips for you:

- Choose a username that is easy to remember.

- Use a recognizable logo or brand photo.

- Focus on using keyword-rich descriptions.

- Don't forget to add a trackable link that leads back to your website.

Share Evergreen Content

The chances are that you might have come across the term "evergreen content" on social media. If not, then it seems that you have not thoroughly engaged in serious social media marketing. A good marketer should always point out to you that one of the secrets to increasing your reach is by posting evergreen content.

So, let's get to the main point: what is evergreen content? Or rather what is evergreen marketing on social media? Simply said, evergreen content refers to the content that would continuously stay fresh regardless of the time posted. In other words, evergreen content will remain relevant to your target market irrespective of the time you posted it. Consequently, something that you posted three or four months ago should remain relevant throughout the year. This strategy also increases your reach if used wisely.

Work smart

An interesting fact about Facebook is that a user is often subjected to more than 1,500 stories in a single day. Therefore, to enhance engagement, users are made only to see 300 of the 1,500 stories. Three hundred of the chosen stories are those that are relevant. What is the point being driven home here? Having more posts on your social media business page doesn't mean that you will reach your audience better. No! Work smart! Understand that relevance matters most. Hence, you should aim to post content that is most relevant to your followers. Again, this takes us back to the importance of understanding your audiences. If you don't know them, there is no way that you will understand what's relevant and what's not.

Post on non-peak hours

I know that this sounds strange, but it certainly works. Posting on non-peak hours is the best way to circumvent all the noise on social media. You might be having some inner voice of discontent about this. Well, think about it this way. When everybody is online, there is a high chance that your target audience will miss your message. There are hundreds of new posts streaming every second. So, if you post during this time, you will miss out the opportunity of increasing your audience. For that very reason, you should wait until everything has calmed down to post relevant content to reach your prospects effectively.

Research shows that the best times to post on Facebook are on Thursday and Friday. Here, you should make your posts from 1 p.m. to 3 p.m. On the other hand, it is best to post on Twitter during the weeks from 12 p.m. to 6 p.m. LinkedIn off-peak times are from Tuesday to Thursday. Between these days, you should post either at 7 a.m. or 8 a.m. Also, you could opt to post in the evening at around 5 p.m. or 6 p.m. Try this, and you will see an increase in your reach.

The Right Content Matters Most

Content will surely make the difference between a good social media marketing campaign and a disastrous one. If you think about this carefully, it would sound pretty apparent to you that content is what people are after when engaging on social media websites. Selling your brand will depend heavily on the content that you use. Why would a customer follow you if at all your content is boring? Customers want to stand out from their friends on social media. They yearn for admiration for their social media activities. This is how celebrities get numerous followers on their social media pages.

For your business, customers will also want something that is worth sticking for. If they are going to tell their friends about you, there should be something good attached to your brand. It is your content. The right content will get you what you want on social media. That's a secret. Take it for free.

With the right content on your page, you can be sure that your audience will be sharing your message all over. You get to indirectly distribute your message through various social media platforms without having to do anything. All you need to do is to make the first post. The rest will be done for you by your audience. They are doing this because you are posting relevant videos, informative videos, inspiring quotes/messages, exciting and engaging photos, etc. Therefore, it is all about using the "social" magic to work on your social media business page.

Marketing Your Social Profile Everywhere

Why should you have a social media business page and yet you cannot market it on your storefront or your business cards? A huge mistake that most business owners make is forgetting the mundane aspects of promoting their social brand. Truly, these are just common marketing factors that might run past our attention. You cannot solely be blamed as there are numerous things to put into consideration when marketing your business over social media platforms. However, when you are busy promoting your business on social media, you should remember that conventional marketing strategies also work.

There are millions of people that still shop from conventional stores. Therefore, this renders these stores as equally important to market your online presence. Design your business cards in a manner that sells your online brand. Some of your customers might not be aware that you have a Facebook account where they can conveniently reach you and make orders. Don't just assume that they prefer shopping from your old store. Give them a reason to think that you are a digitalized business that looks into the future. Your customers expect surprises. This is perhaps the biggest surprise that will transform your business in the long run.

So, the point here is that you ought to focus on marketing your social profile everywhere. Begin by displaying on your storefront and move to your email signatures. As long as you are selling anything, you should be communicating about your online presence. With time, you would be surprised at the number of followers you have.

Engaging With Your Followers for Successful Marketing

The last bit on increasing your social media reach reiterates the message regarding the importance of engaging with your followers. Conventionally, we know how gossip spreads. It spreads like wildfire. Within a short period, good or bad news about your business spreads throughout your community. Well, this is also how social media is. The difference is the rate of spreading. Here, gossip can be shared with millions of people in minutes. Why don't you take advantage of this?

Why don't you take advantage of the fact that your good engagement tactics can sell your brand to millions of people? You will not get a 100% conversion rate. But, you will definitely be overwhelmed with the response rate that you will be receiving on your social media page.

Engaging with your audience decently and making prompt responses to their comments will earn you the gold reputation that you are after. When this happens, rest assured that the news will spread to different social media networks. This is what reach is all about. As a business, you want your brand message to reach out to many people. Expect new visitors to your business website as a product of your outstanding engagement skills.

Chapter 6

"The goal is to provide inspiring information that moves people to action."

-Guy Kawasaki.

Social Media Marketing - Building One on One Relations

When you look at big players in the market that you are operating in, there is a common thing about them. These companies boast of a loyal following capable of sticking with them in good and in bad times. But, how do they get to this point? It is the question that you should be asking yourself. What is it that made these companies have a loyal following?

With more than 1 billion social media users, you might be wondering how a business can get to interact and build one on one customer relations. The truth of the matter is that other companies out there are boasting of loyal customers. This means that it is something attainable. You only need to learn more about the tips and tricks of building and maintaining such one on one customer relationships.

Getting new customers to depend on your brand is not an easy job. Similarly, the same effort goes to retaining the customers that your business has won over. Fortunately, there are proven strategies to handle customers over the internet. The idea of strengthening customer relationships and learning how to retain them aid in enhancing a brand over a certain period.

One of the main challenges that you would incur in building one on one relations with your customers is knowing which strategies to utilize. The strategies that you employ would, in the end, make a massive difference with regards to the trust that your audience would develop about your brand. Here are suggested strategies that would help in customer relationship management.

Proof of care

In any normal relationships that we enter into, our partners always yearn for attention. They crave for attention to the extent that they feel alone when we show that we don't care. Showing care to those that are dear to us is the best way of informing them that they are important to us.

Likewise, in business, this is the same requirement when dealing with customers. Customers crave for attention more so when relating to them over social media pages. An important thing to recall, however, is that customers are out seeking genuine care. They want companies to show them that they genuinely care about their health and wellbeing. Any snarky attitude would bring an air of mistrust. When offering help to your clients on social media, ensure that you are genuine. Your sincere attitude won't go unnoticed as customers would develop trust in your brand.

Regular communication

In line with the concept of engaging with your social media customers on a personal level, clients expect regular communication from your end. An inactive or dormant website will certainly not generate any leads. There is nothing exciting about a social media account where only customers share their complaints only to land on deaf ears.

Therefore, when communicating with customers, it is imperative to respond politely. This applies to both angry and happy customers. Receiving complaints from angry customers does not mean that you are dealing with a lousy product. It only implies that the customers are helping you identify some of the weaknesses that your brand suffers from. Accordingly, it is best that you thank them for being honest.

Visitors to your social media business page will feel at home and welcomed when you take time to respond to them promptly and in the right manner. It gets them engulfed into the conversation. Before they know it, they would be purchasing your product or relying on your service.

Host events

Marketing your business on social media pages is a way of trying to get social with real people and winning them over to depend on your brand. Remember, there are numerous brands out there marketing their brands the same way you are doing. So, standing out is vital. Getting your customers to interact with your brand personally works like magic. Organize events on social media and invite your followers. This can be done either online or offline. Nonetheless, it is recommended that you try combining both strategies for the best results.

Reward your Customers

Rewarding customers is another way in which a business could get to improve the relationships that they have with their customers. A business could choose to reward their regular and loyal customers as a way of showing appreciation. Equally, rewarding customers shows a sign of respect from the business. Business experts would identify this process as giving back to the community.

Consistency is key

Maintaining or strengthening customer relations with your business demands for consistency. The way in which you respond to angry customers today should be similar to how you will react months later. Customers will end up treasuring the fact that your business is always respectful no matter what.

When relating to your customers through the provision of information or simply posting relevant updates, you should remember to be consistent. Consistency will ultimately pave the way for customer retention. A good number of customers out there are loyal to their brands simply because of the consistent quality of services that they get.

Increasing Customer Interest in Your Brand

As customers learn to trust you, there is no doubt that they would be choosing your brand over rival brands in the same industry. However, as you might have noticed, trust is earned. You have to work for it. Good news for you is that there are recommended strategies of winning your customers' trust as well as increasing their interest in the brand you offer them.

Get Visual

The vast world of social media is always surprising. A business owner could spend millions on marketing their brand over social media, and yet it could end up not paying off. What should you do or how do you go about this? First, understand that certain forms of content are considered as more engaging as compared to others. Getting visual content, for example, is an excellent way of capturing your audience's attention. Everybody loves to watch videos. Therefore, it would make a lot of sense if you chose to invest in featuring video posts on your social media business page.

The same thing applies to photos. They are an eye-catcher. As one scrolls down their Facebook page, there is a good chance that they would stop somewhere to catch a glimpse of the photos you posted. On the contrary, they might fail to notice your written content. Hence, think twice about the idea of using visuals to increase customer interest in your brand. Invest wisely in what you know will pay off.

Be Conversational

There are thousands of businesses on social media today. It implies that customers are the ones to choose the best from the lot. Your posting behavior will have an impact on the customers that you would be attracting. Similarly, it will influence the rate at which you influence consumers to opt for your brand as compared to your competitors. As such, it is important not to post outbound messages that will only drive attention away from your brand. Customers are not patient. That is for sure. They are numerous other posts to go through. So, what do you do? Be conversational. Bring up conversations and mention specific customers to capture their attention. You will gain an enhanced engagement level with your clients. More followers will soon follow suit.

Get the right blend of engagement and action

Engagement alone will not guarantee that you get optimum results as you try to increase customer interest in your brand. The engagement strategy that you adopt should be blended with the right action. For example, when engaging with your prospects on YouTube, you should leave behind a call-to-action message. This spurs curiosity amongst your audience.

Make the best of social influencers

Numerous newbie companies seeking to invest in marketing on social media often give up because of the tedious job that is required to build a following from scratch. Well, if you ask those who have been through the process, they would concur that it is laborious and frustrating at the same time.

Fortunately, there is a shortcut that you can take advantage of and get your customers talking about your brand. Using social media influencers does the magic of helping you earn a large following within a short period. Hence, you are saved from the hustle and bustle of having to learn all the basics of social media marketing.

What or who is a social media influencer? You might guess that a social media influencer is an individual with a large following capable of influencing your brand by directly associating with it. Well, it is true. A social media influencer refers to a social media user who boasts of established credibility in a particular industry. They have a large following. Therefore, they can easily persuade their followers, thanks to their established credibility in the industry.

The benefit you gain is that you will attract a large following by basically associating with social media influencers. It is an excellent way of skipping the mundane social media marketing activities and getting things to work for you right away.

Give freely to get freely

It would be selfish of you to expect a lot from your audiences and yet there is nothing you give in return. In this case, you expect that your followers will actively share your content while you go through their posts. It doesn't work that way. To maximize the benefits of engaging with your prospects, give freely the way you are also getting your likes and shares voluntarily. Accordingly, share your audience's content freely whenever possible. Like their posts and subscribe to their channels.

Personalizing the Social Media Experience

Customers are always keen to depend on brands that engage with them directly. These customers are more inclined to do business with businesses that deliver them a personalized social media experience. What does this mean? It means that customers do not want to be treated as customers collectively. They yearn to be treated as individuals.

So, how do you ensure that you create a personalized experience among your audiences?

First, learn from how other rival brands are creating personalized social media experiences with their audiences. Take note of the way these companies are responding to customer queries and attending to them both offline and on social media. For example, if a customer posts a comment that they were happy about a particular service, you should comment by mentioning their specific names. It gives them the feeling that they are talking to human beings. This is the kind of personalized experience that we are talking about.

Some essential tips to help you personalize your marketing experience include the following:

Collect adequate data

The only way that you would be in a position to personalize your social media experience as a business owner is by collecting sufficient data. Data concerning your customer attributes over social media pages will be of great importance when it comes to decision making. The right amount of data will aid you in generating buyer personas that guarantee better content. For example, having sufficient data about your audience on Facebook will help you create targeted Facebook adverts. These ads will match with your audience's needs. Therefore, it transforms into a personalized social media experience.

Create customer personas

Simply stated, this is the process of segmenting your audience. Some of the factors to put into consideration include their age, income, location, gender, complaints, and interests. Creating customer personas gives you the advantage of meeting the needs of individual customer personas. For instance, a company could easily refine their messages to suit the interests of young teens aged 13-18 years. Consequently, creating customer personas is an ideal and recommended way of personalizing social media experience among your audiences.

Craft out your personalized content

Before you mull over other tips of personalizing the social media experience of your audience, you should craft out your personalized content. A good example of how this is done is through emails. If you are sending emails to your clients, ensure that they are personalized to match their needs and preferences. The advantage gained here is that your audience will highly likely find the content as relevant. You must have received emails from some of the brands that you often rely on wishing you a happy birthday. This content is personalized only to you. It is a commendable way of winning over customers' trust.

Personalizing the entire experience

Besides personalizing content, you should also focus on personalizing the entire social media experience. Give your customers the opportunity of accessing your social media business page with the convenience of their smartphones. You can be guaranteed that the personalized experience delivered through their smartphones will leave your audience talking. They will have to comment about the convenience that your brand offers as it can easily be accessed on mobile devices.

Chapter 7

"Without continual growth and progress, such words as improvement, achievement, and success have no meaning"

-Benjamin Franklin.

Fundamentals for Continued Success with Social Media Marketing

Small and large businesses should never hesitate to have solid reasons as to why they are using social media for marketing their products and services. Quite visibly, the main reason for marketing products over social platforms is because the customers are there. Your businesses depend on them for growth, survival, and ultimate success.

However, with the numerous guides that are flooded over the internet, it might be difficult to come across a guide that reveals to you the secrets of maintaining that winning pace. All these guides you have gone through must have detailed how best you can succeed in marketing your business over social media. But, few or none have revealed to you how to continue enjoying success over the long haul. Truth be told, getting to the top is easy. Nevertheless, remaining there is where the challenge begins.

Have you ever wondered why big players in the market engage in extensive marketing campaigns and yet they have proven themselves to be the best? Why are they continuously marketing their brand over social networks? They have already succeeded. So, what is the need for splashing their money on creative content and paying expert marketers?

Take a look at brands like Coca Cola, McDonald, KFC, or Pepsi. These brands never get tired of marketing their brands. They always post ads after ads as though customers are already tired of what they posted the previous day. So, the question is whether it is vital to spend a lot even when the brands are already recognized in the market?

One thing that everybody understands, including your customers, is that marketing is inexorable to the success of your brand. Without marketing, you are doomed to fail. Marketers understand perfectly that marketing is required in all the stages of a product lifecycle. The lifecycle here begins with the introduction of a product/service to the market and ends with a declining phase. At every phase, marketing has to be done. You cannot avoid it in your business. Whether you have monopolized the market or not, you still have to market your brand.

On that note, the following are logical reasons as to why big players in any industry engage in continued social media marketing campaigns.

Sending the message of constant improvement

So, say you have marketed your product on social media, and you have created the right image in the minds of your audiences. This is a good move. Nonetheless, you should not stop there. Ongoing marketing aids in giving your customers the perception that you are continuously making improvements to the product/service that you offer them. Customers easily get enticed by the idea that there is something new about the product that they are using. As a result, they would always rely on your brand. These additional features in your brand pave the way for customer satisfaction.

Growing your customer base

Continued marketing about a product generally increases the customer base over a long period. Depending on the product development phase that your brand is in, it first gets the audience hooked. It is worth noting that this won't last for long if you stop your social media marketing efforts. Keeping up with your marketing campaigns guarantees that you capture other people that have never tried using your product. In the long run, you will expand your customer base.

Taking advantage of multiple options

With the experience that you probably have to this point about social media marketing, you are well aware of the fact that there are many options for your marketing strategies. This means that continued marketing gives you a reason to step back and decide on the best option to take. You get to focus on different marketing strategies that would profit your business. After all, there is no point where you can say that your business is enough. You can never get to the point where you say that your business has enough customers and that you don't need others.

Securing your company's future

The fast-changing world of the internet requires that we continuously evolve as it also changes from day to day. The social media marketing strategies that you use today might be obsolete tomorrow. Companies need to come up with innovative ideas of adding flavor to their brands. They need to stay fresh and on top of the existing competition. So, businesses should strive not to lose their brand appeal in the market. Failing to market is, therefore, a way of killing your business gradually. You should not be surprised if a leading brand in the market comes crumbling down to extinction tomorrow.

So, are you still puzzled about the reasons why big players in the market engage in continued marketing over social platforms regardless of their success? Unquestionably, the reason is made clear. Companies yearn to maintain their brand recognition in their market of operation. Moreover, they also seek to grow their customer base while taking advantage of multiple marketing strategies that are at their disposal. Most importantly, continuous marketing guarantees that they secure their company's future from unforeseen market changes.

Generally, after succeeding in your marketing campaign on social media, you should not stop there. Remember, there are different phases that your product/service goes through. In all these phases, marketing is unavoidable. Perhaps one of the ways to keep motivating yourself is by having the perception that you still have a long way to go. This gives you a reason to try out different social media marketing strategies that boost your business growth rate. In the end, you might find yourself operating as one of the big players in the market.

Social Media Channel Mix and Tactics

The continued success of your business is heavily dependent on the social media marketing strategies that you will be utilizing over the long run. One thing that you should understand is that the right social media mix will make a difference in your long term marketing campaign. Social media mix refers to the process of evaluating the most reliable platforms that would ensure you conduct successful marketing campaigns.

Unquestionably, there are a wide array of platforms that you can choose from to market your brand. Nevertheless, it doesn't mean that you should settle for any. Also, social media mix requires that you combine several social networks that seem to work with the brand that you are offering your customers. For example, you might choose to use Facebook, LinkedIn, and Twitter at the same time. Keep in mind that your decisions to settle for a particular mix are reliant on the social media marketing objectives that you have set.

To maximize the benefits that could be obtained in using the right social media mix, social media marketing experts recommend the following tips:

Create an Ideal Social Media Marketing Mix

When choosing the best social media network, the central idea that you should keep in mind is that your goal is to settle for platforms that are in line with your marketing objectives. Before settling for any platform, ask yourself these questions:

- What purpose does this social platform serve?

- Which audiences does the social platform target?

- How much time is required to invest in the social platform for optimum results?

Getting answers to these questions guarantees that you end up settling for the right platform for your social media marketing campaign. Some of the most important factors to consider when choosing the best platform have been discussed in this material. You should refer to the mentioned tips as making the right choice is a fundamental requirement for the success of your business.

To help you make a valid choice, below is a brief look at the top social media networks to use in creating an ideal social media mix.

Facebook
Relevant traits:
Facebook stands as one of the most popular social networks that we have today. This is a platform that is often used by individuals of almost all ages. Due to its diversity, any company can utilize Facebook to market its products. The best part is that it is considered to have an admirable

engagement rate. This means that your customers will regularly interact thereby increasing the chances of your brand being accessible.

Purpose:

Facebook, as a social network, provides brands with an opportunity of building a good reputation among its audiences. Moreover, it helps in promoting customer loyalty.

Unique benefits:

- Facilitates a wide market reach with a single post

- It stimulates dialogue and deepens on relevant subjects that suit your business

- Gives an opportunity to increase website traffic

Age: The average age of Facebook users ranges from 25 to 45 years.

Twitter
Relevant traits:

A good number of Twitter users are young individuals aged around 20 years. They represent a group of young people with diverse interests. The continuous flow of tweets on Twitter means that a user is required to post more often. This is the best way to confirm that your audience sees you.

Purpose: Showing quick updates and breaking news. It mainly encourages new content and delivers prompt reactions from your target market.

Unique benefits:

- Users can index their posts using hashtags

- Enables quick tracing of information, for example, recent stories associated with specific companies

- Generates dialogue with real people hence could help in building brand loyalty
- Gives an opportunity to increase website traffic

Age: The average age of Twitter users ranges from 18 to 39 years.

Instagram
Relevant traits:

Research shows that Instagram users are mostly under 30 years of age. There is an even gender distribution among its users. Instagram's success stems from the fact that it is optimized for use on mobile handsets.

Purpose: It is an excellent platform to share visual stories. Therefore, it generates quality interactions as compared to rival social networks.

Unique benefits:

- Ideal platform for visual stories
- Users could index their posts using hashtags
- Delivers a high interaction rate due to its visual content
- Users could easily share content to other social media networks

Age: Most Instagram users are aged 30 and below.

From the look of things, different social media pages would vary with regard to their traits and purpose. Also, the anticipated benefits of these social media pages tend to differ. What does this tell you? When choosing the best social platform to rely on, it is essential to consider their attributes. Take time to study the different forms of social media networks at your disposal. Once you have gathered the right facts, choose the right social media mix that is promising.

So, the right social media mix is not all about listening to the hype going on around you. The mere fact that other businesses make the most out of Facebook does not mean that it would also work for you. Keep in mind that these social pages also vary in content. For example, Instagram's content is unique from Facebook and Twitter. Hence, you might want to go over the objectives of your social media marketing campaign before making any blind moves.

Researching On Existing Competition

Enjoying the success of social media marketing in the long run demands that you research about your competitors. Keeping track of their progress gets you on the know as you would be confident that you are doing the right thing. In as much as you wish to stand out in your market of operation, watching what your competitors are doing is vital. It doesn't mean that you should directly copy their marketing strategies. NO! The point here is the competitors act as a benchmark. If they are doing something unique from what you are doing, then it means you need to adjust your strategies.

The last thing that you need is to be easily faced off from the market only because you were ignorant of your competitor moves. This applies mostly to new market entrants that seek to continue enjoying the fruits of marketing their businesses over social media platforms. Smaller companies could get overwhelmed in the process of trying to match the existing competition in the market. To be on the safe side, it is advisable to watch your competitors and adjust your social media marketing strategies accordingly.

How do you go about researching your competition to guarantee that you know how to anticipate competitor moves?

Broaden your search

Most people would opt to use Google to kick off their search regarding the existing competition that they are facing in the market. While this might be a great place to begin, you should think outside the box. There are numerous tools out there which could help you in gaining insights regarding the competition that you are facing. Some tools that could help you learn more about your competition include Google Alerts, Google Trends, and SpyFu.

Rely on reports

If you are thinking about opting for inexpensive ways of monitoring your competition, then choosing to follow reports could be a good idea. Subscribe to reliable feeds that report on industry trends you operate in. Most of these feeds will tell you a lot about what your rival companies are planning to do. When these reports get to the internet, you can be sure that you will anticipate your competitor moves strategically. For example, if you get a report about the gaps that your rivals are not filling, this could be an excellent way of winning the market over. What you need to do is to embark on an intensive marketing strategy that will inform people out there about your brand and its associated benefits.

Make use of social networks

As you study the existing competition surrounding your brand, you should not overlook the power of social media. Going through Facebook, Twitter, LinkedIn, and Instagram could give you a few tips about what your competitors have been doing. There are mentions here and there about them. This will tell you a lot about what customers are saying about them. If there is something that they are not doing, rest assured that social networks are a great place to find out. Because customers are always behind the curtains, there are no secrets kept in social media. The best part is that there are cost-effective and efficient tools that will make the entire process relatively easy. All you need to do is to understand which ones to choose.

Rely on your customers

Researching about your competitors requires that you sought out information from all corners, including your customers. Whether you opt to use social media or communicate with them directly, getting information from them is very easy. Just ask your customers about the former brands that they have been using. This is a direct question that is not rude to the customer. In fact, any customer would want you to know about their past experiences with other alternative brands.

Wait! Don't ignore your dissatisfied customers. Make a point of asking them about the reasons as to why they opted for rival products. This information should alert you about the things that your brand might be lacking. Hence, you could adjust accordingly to meet customer demands in the future.

Ask your suppliers

Information about your rival companies could also be obtained by talking to suppliers. They know what your competitors are doing to differentiate their products in the market. They can also help you in knowing precisely other additional products that your competitors plan to introduce in the market. Clearly, they may not surrender to you all the information at once.

Nevertheless, if you regularly interact with them, they will surely spill the beans at one point. With this information at hand, you can easily anticipate your competitor moves and adjust accordingly. For instance, you could formulate social media marketing objectives that counter their moves.

From the look of things, researching about your competition in an important factor that guarantees your business thrives. Knowing what you expect from your competitors keeps you ahead of the game. They will always wonder how easily you outperform them regardless of their marketing efforts. Experts would say that it is important to work smart instead of working hard. Well, it doesn't mean that you should not work hard. The idea here is that learn from the best and stay ahead of them. Doing this warrants that you survive in your market of operation for an extended period. Undeniably, your continued success is heavily reliant on what your competitors are doing to counter competition from your end. Therefore, you should make an effort to play your cards right and stand out from the rest through the insights that you learn about your rivals.

Final Thoughts

On a final note, there is no form of 21st-century marketing techniques that can beat the power of social media. Picture a scenario where a single post could be shared with thousands of people in a matter of seconds. This is how fast the news spread over social media channels. Platforms such as Twitter, Facebook, Instagram, and LinkedIn are therefore excellent marketing channels to take advantage of. You ought to commend yourself for digging deeper to find out the best strategies to utilize in marketing your brand over social media.

Today, businesses realize that they cannot counter competition in their industries without the use of social media platforms. Interestingly, micro companies have the same perception. As big companies are competing for their online spaces, smaller companies are also doing the same. After all, they say, "if you can't beat them, join them." So, companies are doing their best to counter competition by simply making use of social platforms as a way of reaching out to their clients.

From what you have learnt in this material, there are numerous social media platforms that you can choose from. However, you shouldn't settle for anyone. This is a huge mistake that most businesses are making. Moreover, having a social media page on all platforms does not mean that your online presence is well covered. In fact, it is quite likely that you might be confusing yourself. The chances are that you might end up failing as you lack the expertise in marketing your product over social media.

To be on the safe side, the first thing that you need to do is to learn the art of it. How are people marketing their products on Facebook? Is it the same with how other companies are selling their brand on Twitter? The nitty-gritty aspects of marketing on social media should be on your fingertips before you think about setting up a social media business page.

The other thing that you should always be keen on is the varying attributes of the specific social media pages. Facebook is different from Instagram or YouTube. Marketing tactics vary across all platforms. This means that having a "one size fits all" policy will render your marketing efforts useless. It is essential to gain an understanding of the different features of every social media page. These features should be matched with your marketing objectives. Doing this ensures that you work smart as you would be using a few social media pages and getting the most out of them.

Always remember to have a plan. Failing to plan is just planning to see your business go into extinction. If you do not know how to plan, learn from what your competitors around you are doing. They are investing here and there on the most reliable social media pages. But what is the secret behind it? Your rival brands have a plan, and they stick to it. In this case, you need to take the time to audit your social media presence before moving further. Find out the platforms that generate more leads for your business. Where is your audience posting their tweets and Facebook posts regularly? Get to know what your customers want to see? Understanding your clients is key to winning them over. It guarantees that you deliver as per their expectations and beyond. Sweeping them off their feet leaves them talking about you. When this happens, you can be confident that your business would be trending within a short period.

If you are planning to go out and just promote your brand on social media, it is best that you think of something else. Marketing on social media is all about getting social. Your customers are out there in varying social networks socializing with each other. This implies that you should also be doing the same thing. Probably you have heard of the phrase "join the community." Yes, being part of social media demands that you join the social community. Meet with your customers on a personal level on Facebook, LinkedIn, or Instagram. Listen to them. What are they saying about your product or services? Are they happy? Are they impressed with the recent changes you made? Or are they in need of a particular service or product that you currently are not offering? Well, listening is key to winning the trust of your clients. It gifts you the knowledge that you need to market your brand over social media effectively.

With regards to monitoring, always monitor your performance regularly. Know where your brand lies in the minds of your consumers. Undeniably, you do not want to be an "option B" in the market. Therefore, make use of the right monitoring tools that work for you. It is recommended that you go through different reviews about these tools before choosing any. It ensures that you end up picking the best from the lot.

Content! Content! Content! This is an area that you MUST improve. Big brands in the market are always at their frontline in making sure that their content is unbeatable. Try your level best to make sure that your content is also relevant. Customers on social media fancy the idea of being associated with brands that post relevant content. If you think that you are not witty enough, just keep it simple. And if possible, hire an expert to do the job for you. Content is what will sell your brand out there. It defines what you are doing, and what you are offering your customers. Therefore, knowing what sells matters a lot to the success of your business.

In line with content, this goes hand in hand with knowing your customers. Without an in-depth knowledge about your customers, you will never know the right content that suits them. So, do your homework. Research about them and their online shopping behaviors. This tells a lot about what they anticipate from your brand.

Before you forget, remember to take note of what your competitors are doing. Their actions could be regarded as a blueprint to what you should be doing. This applies mostly to smaller business in the market. Try to stay unique. But don't be the odd one out.

Taking everything into account, marketing on social media is not challenging. It is also not easy. Therefore, a business owner should invest their time and money in learning the art of it. Getting to know more about social media marketing basics will make a huge difference to your business both in short and in the long run. A working strategy that is worth bearing in mind is that companies should learn from the best. Why? It is the only surest way of also becoming the best in the market.

Good Luck!

Book 2: Content Marketing: Growth Strategies to Stay Ahead in the Changing World of Content Marketing and Maximize ROI.

Book Summary:

Do you want to kick-off your successful content marketing business? As a writer, you can enter the lucrative world of content marketing and secure a successful, high-income career.

Writers used to earn pennies. Today, everyone needs good writing. It's a commodity that has made content marketers high in demand. If you can learn how to create content that performs for your clients, you'll never be without work again. Better yet, you'll earn more than doctors do!

In *Content Marketing,* I will teach you the system that will take you from zero to high flyer in the world of content marketing. Learn to apply your writing skills in the marketing arena, and you will be amazed at the results you can get. This is the career you've been waiting for!

In this step-by-step guide you'll learn:

- How exactly to build an amazing opt-in offer

- Where the money is and how to get it

- How to create the right content, then 10X your results

- To understand what it takes to be a great copywriter

- How to build fantastic landing pages that sell things like hot cakes

- How to market content on Facebook for wider reach

With this all-in-one get-started guide, you'll unpack the most direct route to becoming a competent, in-demand content marketing writer – in just a few days.

Get into content marketing when you apply the tried and tested tips in this guide. There's no time like right now to begin your new, lucrative career!

Become a content marketing superstar with this easy guide.

Buy it now and start writing!

Introduction

"In the middle of every difficulty lies opportunity."

– Albert Einstein

Many businesspeople underplay the role of content marketing in their marketing strategy. This can be a costly error. The message is at the core of any good marketing campaign; understand the way that prospects read their email and you can create a message that will gain and hold their attention, boosting response rates to new levels.

With a little inside knowledge and a little work, you can make a major impact on the income you can generate from your list.

Let's say you have a list of 1,000 subscribers and are currently converting on your email at a rate of 3%. You're getting 20 interested customers. If 50% of them buy a product that nets you $45, then you have made $675. Now imagine that you have adjusted your email marketing copy and bump that conversion rate to 8%. Given the same scenario, you have made $1,800! If you just move that conversion rate up 2 percentage points to 5%, you still boost your income by $450 in that scenario.

Use the 50 tips in this report to fine-tune your email content marketing skills to make your customers/prospects/subscribers more loyal and responsive, and your marketing list more profitable.

Your content doesn't have to be long, it doesn't have to have glossy post-production, or be overly complicated. It *does* need to be interesting and useful, and it *does* have to be engaging and visible. The content you produce should give away the farm. Don't hold anything back from your audience; let them see exactly how you do business, what your processes and perspectives are, and show them that you're a real authority by sharing everything you know.

Chapter 1
Build an Opt-In Offer

"Success is walking from failure to failure with no loss of enthusiasm."

-Winston Churchill

If you spend much time online, particularly in internet marketing circles, you can't avoid hearing about the 'powers' of content marketing. To hear some people talk about it, you would think they'd found the fountain of youth and a vault full of money right beside it… but content on its own is just not enough. Yes, it's powerful because it can cut through the noise online and show your visitors that you can be trusted. But if you're going to build a relationship with those visitors, you've got to have a way to continue communicating with them regularly. You can't assume they'll remember to check your blog every week or that they'll buy from you unprompted.

Most content is distributed on platforms you do not own — Facebook, Twitter, content networks, search engines, and so on. Those platforms own the traffic, and if they change how they do business, you can lose your audience. That's why it's critical to start building a contact list that you own and can market to directly. This is where opt-in offers come into play. Whenever a new person visits your site, they should have the opportunity to join your mailing list or private community in exchange for some incentive. You need to get their email address or have them set up an account so that you can build up a profile for them over time, communicate with them directly, and make carefully targeted sales offers to them when the time is right.

Your opt-in offers do not need to be cripplingly complex. This is a critical aspect of a content marketing strategy, so let me be clear: done is better than perfect. Assets like this can always be more detailed, have a longer word-count, or be more testimonial-heavier, but once you have a good piece of information that's useful, polished and appealing, publish it. Every day that you do not have an active opt-in is a day that you are losing leads, and are wasting the resources you've put into creating your content so far. Ideally, you would give the subscriber a piece of premium content, but at the very least, a pop-up box that asks for their email address will do (use SumoMe.com to get that set up).

Here are some asset types for compelling opt-in offers:

- Industry report or white paper

- Case study

- Video series

- Webinar

- Demo

- Discount code

- Quiz or survey

- Cheat sheet

- How-to guide

- Industry or client profiles

Pick the type of asset most appropriate to your industry, and based on what your customers will value. Make sure that it's better information than they would usually find within your public content, and make it feel high-quality wherever possible so that they're impressed and want to see what comes next. The offer should also have a clear benefit for the subscriber: take care to communicate the value they are going to get as a result of giving you their information, and that you set their expectations accurately before they opt in. Make sure the asset is delivered to them immediately, via a thank-you page and/or a confirmation email.

Build an Onboarding Sequence

Getting someone's email address or having them create an account is a big win. This is a micro-commitment from them (which is the first step towards having them buy from you), as well as getting their permission to market to them. This is huge, and you want to capitalize on this opportunity. An email onboarding sequence creates a window for you to do that. Onboarding, also referred to as 'organizational socialization', is done through an automated sequence of emails by which subscribers are educated about your brand, engaged with your community, and indoctrinated with your values.

Here's a templated structure you can use for a general onboarding sequence. If someone has opted in to receive something, these are some general topics for the emails you might send them:

(We'll go into further depth on how to build your onboarding sequences later on in this book.)

The goal of this sequence is to establish yourself as an authority on the topic they opted in to hear about and to get them to take the next step with you. Whether it's booking a call, taking a demo, joining a webinar, or even just replying to an email, make sure you're positioning the subscriber to engage. This is mission-critical. People need to be led, so make sure you have something specific you are leading them towards. You never want someone to be unclear about what their next step should be. This is true at any point as the customer is moving through your ecosystem, but *particularly* at this stage when they've been exposed to your ideas and expertise, and it's time for them to make a purchasing decision.

Depending on the nature of your market, your offering, and the messaging that works best, common 'next steps' in a B2B business would be one of the following:

• Invite them to a free webinar. A lot of marketers do this extremely well — people like Frank Kern, Noah Kagan, and Ryan Levesque leverage webinars to engage people to great success all the time. This format works so well because it allows the marketer to give a lot of value up front, without requiring a large time investment from the prospect. Webinars are also a direct platform to sell from, as they basically create a captive audience: the prospect joins the webinar, learns lots of good stuff, and then (with the principle of reciprocity working quietly in the back of their mind) will sit through a sales pitch even if they don't have to. At this point, the prospect is primed: they think of you as an approachable authority who is speaking directly to their problems, and so you can offer them your solution while they are right there in a receptive frame of mind.

• Offer them a free demo. This works similar to the webinar model but works particularly well for SaaS (software as a service) businesses and companies that offer some kind of technical solution. We built a free demo offer into the onboarding email sequence for Wicked Reports, and they saw a significant uptick in both booked demos and sales. Having some prior education about the product, their prospects become very curious to see the tool in action in a few different scenarios, and are therefore willing to book in an hour to get to know Wicked Reports better. Most people learn well in a visual format, so seeing the tool in use is a powerful way to move them towards a conversion. Do you know the old saying "possession is nine-tenths of the law"? Well, an interactive demo is about as close as you can get to having the prospect 'possess' the product. If you can demonstrate your offer in action, they're going to be much more likely to take the next step you want.

• Invite them to a free call. This works particularly well for consultants and service businesses because often the offer is a little less tangible than what's being sold by other B2B businesses. Make it clear that it's an obligation-free call, and that they can spend as much time as they want to ask questions, picking apart your offer, and really getting a feel for whether you're the right fit for them. It's an opportunity for them to air any skepticism, get clarity about what they need, and get to know you. A very powerful part of the onboarding process is that they get sufficiently educated about your product or process so that they feel comfortable getting on the phone with you because they will then know what they're talking about. You never want someone to come into a conversation this blind, because the power balance is too much in your favor. In that situation, the prospect can feel that you hold all the cards and they don't have enough information to assess whether you're being straightforward with them. This makes people feel defensive, and wary of you trying to 'put it over them'. You want to make sure they have a locus of control in the interaction so that they're comfortable and more open to the conversation. Before getting on the phone with anyone, make sure they have as much information as they need, and let them know that you encourage a critical approach in your customers, that you only want to work with people who take their business seriously, and that you're not going to put a hard sell on them.

All the content that you produce up to this point should be driving the prospect towards having some kind of real-time interaction with you. Business is about people, and people won't do anything if trust and rapport is missing from an interaction. They need to relate to you as a person they can trust; a person who will be a positive influence in their business, and will ultimately help them fill whatever deep-seated need is driving them.

(And make no mistake — it's rarely a cut and dry desire to make more money that drives people. Some want status, others want recognition, others still want positive feedback... there's a whole neurochemical chain reaction going on when someone makes a buying decision, and while that's beyond the scope of this book, we'll be getting into a little bit of the behavioral psychology that should factor into your marketing later on.)

Carlos Ruiz Zafón, one of the most popular Spanish novelists of the modern age, says that we only accept as true what can be narrated. Knowing, then, that people will only buy what you're selling when it's wrapped up in a story or narrative that resonates with them - you need to find a way to position your content in a way that does that. Your offer should be presented as a story they can see themselves taking an active part in, and you, yourself should be presented as a narrator they trust and find relatable.

Understanding that, you should always be driving them to some sort of interactive action. This is a critical aspect of high-converting content: there's always a clear call to action that moves them further through your funnel. The prospect is never left alone without a clear next step; they'll never wonder if you have some hidden ulterior motive — they know and trust you because you told them the story they needed to hear. This is why knowing deeply who your audience is, what offer they need to receive, and how to position your messaging, is the cornerstone of creating high-converting content.

Next, we're going to dive into the two most critical steps of all — making sales offers and following up with your prospects.

Make Sales Offers

The secret to creating content that converts is to create a conversion moment. Yes, despite all the progress that marketing has made, you still have to make sales offers if you want to convert your prospects. No marketing system in the world can extract a sale without first making a sales offer.

All businesses live and die by the number of sales they make. It doesn't matter how good your systems are, or if you have a great team, or you've got unrivalled SOPs… it doesn't even matter if you have hyper-focused marketing and a replicable lead acquisition funnel. If you don't make sales offers, it's all for nothing.

Of the dozens of B2B businesses I've worked with over the years, just one thing separates the success stories from the failures, and it's that the leaders of the company committed to sales. They committed to making the offer every time — they committed to ignoring their fear of rejection, their anxiety about pissing people off, and the voice in their head that said they couldn't do it. They committed, consistently made their offers, and came out on top because of it.

Sales offers come in all shapes and sizes, depending on the business. You might invite someone to book a paid consult with you, or you might offer them an ongoing service for which they pay you every month. You might offer them the purchase of a single unit, or the purchase of thousands of units. You might offer them paid access to a piece of software that will automate part of their business. Whatever it is, you need to explicitly offer to give them your product or service in return for a specific amount of money.

If you are afraid of making sales offers off the back of your content, or you 'sell from your heels' (making a half-hearted attempt at a sale that doesn't really showcase the benefits, or ask the prospect for an answer), your content will never convert a single customer. You will be wasting all your resources and in time, your business will fail.

- Being 'uncovered' as a fraud

- Being rejected

- Being found lacking in either their qualifications or what they're offering

- Being perceived as pushy, rude, or mercenary

- Being unable to deliver what they are offering

Usually, these fears are completely unfounded, and they're all rooted in the fundamental human need to be accepted by your tribe. It's horrible to think that someone you pitch would be offended by your offer, and then go and rip on you all over the internet... but with a content ecosystem that gradually entices people to your offer, and sharing information that benefits them and shows that you have their best interests in mind, you're not going to get that kind of treatment.

The great thing about the content ecosystem is that most of the people you will speak to will be pre-qualified as a potential buyer, so they're likely to respond positively to an offer. The best approach, in this case, is usually not a hard sell, but a simple mention of 'here's what I've got, here's what it will do for you, and here's how to get it.'

In fact, I've never had a client have a bad reaction from their customers when they make their sales offer at the end of a content funnel. I've never had a bad reaction for my own services, either. That doesn't mean bad reactions can't happen — selling is both art and science, and you *can* get it wrong, but if you are putting your customers first then you can feel confident that you'll usually get a good response.

If need be, practice your sales offers. Get a friend or colleague on the phone, or in however method you will be making pitches to customers, and practice on them. It's worth the awkwardness and will pay a huge ROI on the time and energy you spend on it. Ideally, your practice partner will actually fit your primary customer profile. Give them your onboarding material to read first, so that they come to the practice sales situation with all the same knowledge your real prospects will have. Go through the process of the onboarding event — whether it's a webinar, demo or call — and then transition into your sales offer.

Practice moving the conversation from the free content to the sales offer. Practice your positioning, and how you talk about the offer. Practice the language that works best to communicate all the benefits of the offer, and practice how to overcome objections by encouraging your partner to come up with as many as they can, based on what you've already discussed. Finally, find out from them what questions went unanswered for them during the process, what objections they kept to themselves, and what would have made them commit to the sale that you didn't address. Try to get a real-world interaction that will emulate the sales process for you, so that when you do it with real prospects, you're in familiar territory.

Never pass up the opportunity to make a sale. If you have someone on a call, or in some kind of interaction with you, do not put it off. Do not say to yourself *"I'll just send them an email that closes them after this"* or *'they'll tell me if they want to go ahead with something"*. No, you won't, and no, they won't. Unless you have explicitly promised not to sell them anything, always be selling.

(The only time you should ever promise not to sell during an interaction is when you need something from the prospect other than the sale, like early market feedback. Otherwise, avoid making promises that will prevent you from making money.)

Be as generous and fully present as you can be during the sales process. Answer every question honestly and with your full attention. Dig into their doubts, invite them to hit you with their best shot — make them understand that you *really* care about their situation and are helping them to find the right solution. Before they get off the call, get a yes or no answer from the prospect. Just ask: *"Are you ready to go ahead?"* No maybes, or let-me-think-about-its. Yes or no. If they push back on you, simply say that you want to get a specific answer from them so you know how to move forward with them. It might sound aggressive, but when positioned correctly, this is a powerful method to make sure that all the content you've produced so far actually does the job and makes people convert.

Chapter 2
The Money Is in The Follow-Up

"The most unprofitable item ever manufactured is an excuse."

– John Mason

This is the most important principle you can learn in marketing. It's rare that a visitor will convert on their first visit to your site, or that even a warm prospect will convert at their first point of contact with you. Of course, if your initial onboarding funnel does a great job of orienting them into your business and demonstrating your value, you might have a pretty good conversion rate right out of the gate. But for most companies (particularly those making high price-point offers) getting the conversion can take a few interactions. People want to get to know the way you approach the industry, that you're a trustworthy and legitimate company, and that other people have successfully done business with you.

Now, assuming that your prospects have gone through each part of the ecosystem, they should know, like, and trust you. They should understand the benefits of what you're offering, and they should understand your perspective on the industry. If they haven't bought from you yet, then it's time to bring a follow-up system to life so that all your hard work helps get them past the tipping point, rather than indefinitely hovering around it.

If someone says no when you make your sales offer, here's what you do. You tell them that you are going to send them a recap of your conversation, so that they can reply with any questions that come to them afterwards, and that you're going to follow up with them in a few weeks (and make sure it goes on your calendar to do so). When you follow up with them as promised, you'll often find that they have made no progress towards their stated goals. This is where you can restate their exact motivation for speaking with you and highlight how you can help them: *"Here's the offer I made you last time. Here's the way I can make it even better for you, so you can stop wasting time and start seeing the progress you need: [insert offer here of a discount, done-for-you element, additional features, bonuses, etc]."*

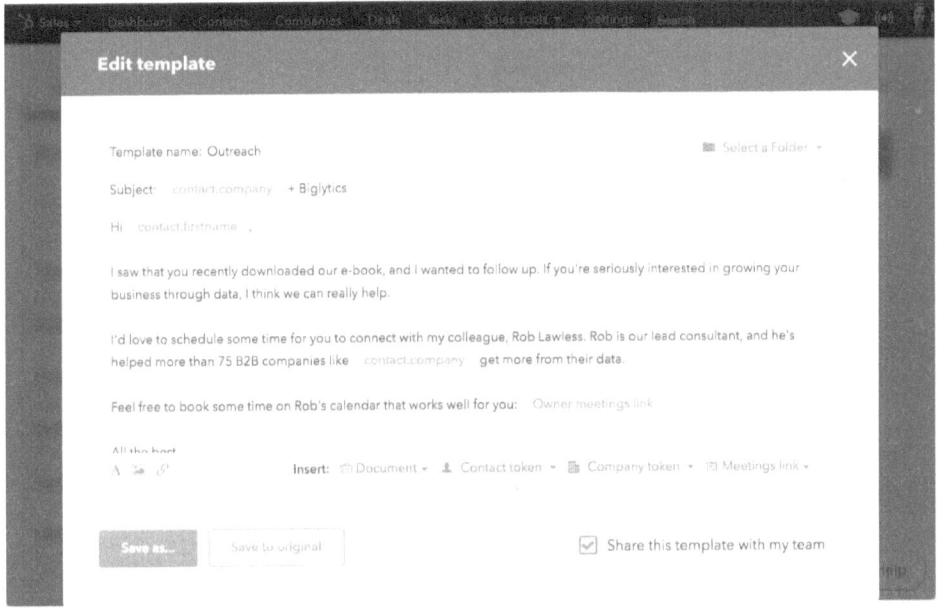

Figure 1.

Alternately, if you would rather automate your follow-up, you can build out two email funnels to do all this work for you: one funnel for people who converted, and one for people who have not converted yet, using the same process you used to build your onboarding email funnel. The funnel for people who do convert should include welcome material, next steps for them to get started with you, and bonus content. For people who have not converted yet, provide more educational and useful content, and keep inviting them to conversion opportunities.

Figure 2.

Content assets are long-form pieces of content that you can use to attract high-end clients, by demonstrating that you are an authority and that you have an uncommon depth of knowledge in your industry. Sharing your expertise in a generous, transparent way like this is a powerful way to get your business in front of big clients who could change the game for you.

In your content asset, you really pull back the curtain on your expertise, writing the playbook on how your clients could implement your custom strategies to solve their problems.

It sounds like giving away your secret sauce, but in reality, people just want to taste the sauce and know how you make it, rather than making the sauce themselves. The ingredients for Sriracha Hot Sauce are listed in detail on Wikipedia, but no one wants to make it themselves. They want to buy that bottle with the rooster on it and have it ready to go without having to find all the specialty grocers, get the right balance of ingredients, and then sweat it out in the kitchen themselves. It's the same with your process: people are curious about the details, but they really just want the result without having to do the work themselves.

ViperChill is just one business that provides a great example of this. The owner, Glen Allsopp, regularly produces incredibly valuable long-form content about SEO on his blog. He doesn't withhold any key information or force you to opt-in to get this content. He shares everything that's been working for his selection of SEO-drive niche websites, big upcoming opportunities in the industry, as well as transparent updates about the progress of his business. Far from costing him work, Glen gets to be totally selective about his client roster — his expertise and generosity show that he's the best in the business, and so the best in *other* businesses line up to work with him.

The big win, of course, is that pulling back the curtain like this makes you look like a giant. It implies that it doesn't matter to you if people do it themselves, or even if your competitors steal your system — your business is so robust and you have so much confidence in your process that you can easily afford for that to happen. It's an attractive attitude to clients who want to work with the best in the field.

The most common content assets used in B2B businesses are books and training courses. Any large piece of content you create that will hold its value and separate you from the market is a content asset. I'm going to use books as my key example throughout this section, as that's what I specialize in, but all this information applies just as well to training courses and other long-form assets.

Creating a content asset and building a strategy around it is not the right move for all businesses. E-commerce companies, for example, are generally better served by recurring content. Businesses with low price-point products also do better with recurring content — there's a much lower barrier to purchase among the audience, and creating a long-form asset may be overkill. But if your business sells high-ticket items or services, then a content asset is a powerful demonstration of authority and credibility. It can shortcut the process of winning trust and confidence from potential clients and is an incomparable differentiator from your competitors.

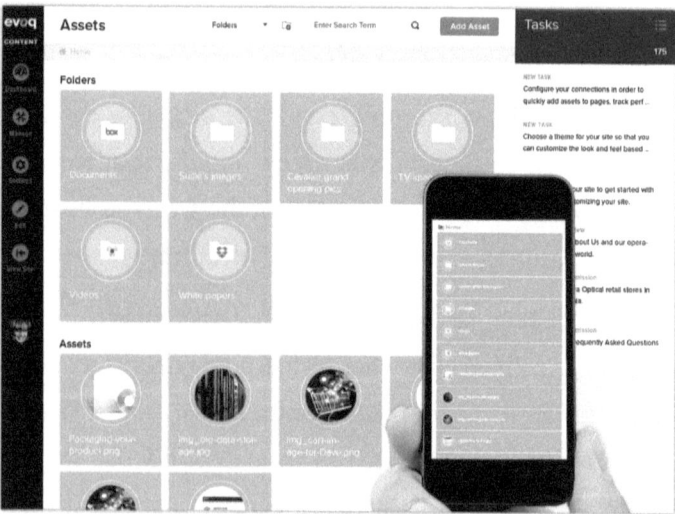

Figure 3.

It requires a massive effort to build this kind of content asset. If you are running your own business, finding the time to write every day is going to be tough — particularly to get to the kind of word count that makes publishing a book worthwhile. And once you decide to write a book, speed to market becomes important, so that you're not beaten to the punch by a competitor with the same idea.

All the people for whom I've ghostwritten books have been met with this exact problem: they have too much to do in their businesses to make real progress on their book each day. They realize that if it's going to happen, someone else needs to take the lead. Where they can produce 300 or 500 words a day, a good professional writer can produce 3000 to 5000 words a day... and when you're writing a book with a 40,000 or 50,000-word count, the difference in timeline is massive.

What usually decides it for them, though, is that the book needs to be marketed *at the same time* it is being written. If you are going to create real momentum for your business with your book, it needs to launch to fanfare and blanket coverage where your primary customers are going to see it (not to launch to crickets and then slowly build up a following over time). The business owner has the connections and positioning to make that happen, but they can't do that and write the damn thing at the same time. They hand the legwork off to me and then focus instead on getting it in front of the right people. Even if you have a dedicated audience who will be supportive, you want to be seeding their interest, getting early purchasing commitments from them, and having them commit to sharing it for you when the time comes.

That element — getting it in front of the right people — is the most critical part of producing a content asset. You want to use it to attract higher value customers, and as a way to 'rack the shotgun' to get the attention of people who are serious about solving the problem you specialize in. The people who are willing to read a book about your solution are often going to be the same people who are willing to pay an expert to take care of it for them — when you're thinking about creating an asset like this, you need to think of it with your future sales system in mind.

Content hackers can always change their minds, but the marketing-plan mindset is inflexible because it lives and dies by the words, charts, and mission statements chiseled on those fifty-two sheets of paper.

For the marketing-plan marketer, once you make the plan, you work it. That's not how it works for the content hacker. And if you suitably increase your tolerance for failure, you're ready to put unheard-of methodologies to work for you - the things that "just aren't done!" This is how you can 10x your business—and in short order.

What will content hacking look like for you?

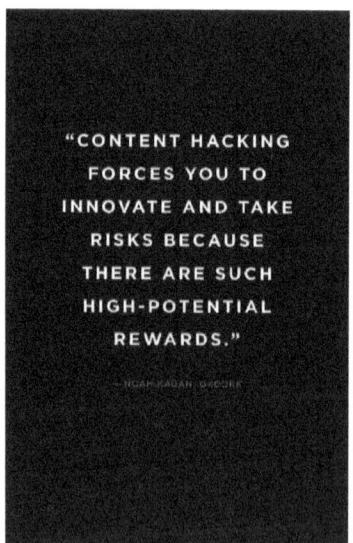

Figure 4.

10x Marketing Interview: Noah Kagan and the Proactive Dashboard

Content hacking forces you to innovate and take risks because there are such high-potential rewards. However, with innovation and risk comes failure - and lots of it.

The Proactive Dashboard

According to Noah, most of your growth attempts aren't going to work. This is why he's adopted a framework for growth that systematically tests ideas, keeping the winners and chucking the duds. His team at Sumo documents does these tests using what they call proactive dashboards.

Each week, their teams test a fresh idea and track its results on their dashboard. That means they test fifty-two new ideas each year. From content to ads to email, they're constantly testing. Noah says the regular routine of testing promotions forces his team to find the stuff that works.

Imagine what that would look like for your company. How innovative would you get if you forced each marketing team—or even team member—to test a never-before-tried method each week? This kind of consistent innovation fosters growth and helps avoid the copycat marketing trap.

Here's the thing, though. In the last four months, only two tests have worked. In fact, 86 percent of Sumo's tests haven't worked. So, if you have more than two out of ten attempts succeed, you're sitting pretty. And rather than be depressing, that statistic should actually be encouraging. Failure is the nature of the beast. But every time you learn what doesn't work, it allows you to kill it and allows room for finding something that does work.

Building Out the Dashboard

To begin, every item on the dashboard has to be fully controllable by you and your team. This means that you cannot be dependent upon anything outside of your activities. The problem is that most of the metrics we're looking at as marketers have already happened. So, this dashboard isn't simply based upon past results you cannot change. It's proactive in that it's filled with goals you can influence right now.

This is a living dashboard that's updated live. Then, as you move forward, you measure against the secondary metric you're hoping to impact. If it doesn't move the needle, you stop doing it. But if it does, it's a keeper.

Noah explains, "We have two proactive dashboards. We have one for Sumo.com and one for each business unit. The idea, and the reason I love them is that everything has to be completely controllable by you. What does that mean? It means you can't be dependent on anything . . . The dashboard is solely the things we have full control of each week. It's a live-tracking, living dashboard."

Sumo has a proactive dashboard for each marketing team. Here's a breakdown of their dashboards for two of their teams, advertising, and content:

Advertising

Advertising has to spend a certain amount, which is completely in their control. This means they can run as many ad variations as they want within their budget. Each week, they spend $7,560 and run at least five variations.

Key Takeaway: What can you directly control and measure in real time?

Content

The content team measures how many pieces of content they publish per week. And on this content, they test things like headlines, email opt-ins, marketing promotion tests, and promotional ad spend. For instance, they tested five weekly posts on Quora for each week. After measuring, however, they saw only 1,000 visitors from each post—which for their team did not merit continuing. The team decided this when they compared it to LinkedIn, which was getting ten times the results Quora was.

Key takeaway: What can you stop doing today that isn't generating results?

Defining and Understanding Your Target Audience

Implicit in the activities of content hacking is a target audience to which you tailor your content. This makes defining and deeply understanding your ideal customer paramount. For Sumo, this was an evolutionary process. As they grew, so did their understanding of who best benefited from their product.

To do this, the Sumo team looked at which customers churn the least, have the highest lifetime value and are easiest for their sales team to talk to and close deals with. They then worked backward from this group, which made their target audience much more obvious.

They noticed that huge publishers like the New York Times were a tough sell. Alternatively, small solo bloggers were also tough because they had such a small budget, and their tiny cash flow made them averse to paying for tools. After some fine-tuning and research, however, they found that e-commerce customers were their sweet spot. Why? Because they could directly achieve ROI in proportion to email list growth. In other words, if they could grow their email list by a factor of ten, they could multiply their customer base in the same way.

For Noah, this changed their entire approach to marketing and content. Originally, their blog was all about getting more traffic - this was a fine goal at the beginning. And for other marketers, it's a perfect metric when traffic correlates to revenue or whatever their goal outcome is. However, even as Sumo's content team tripled their traffic, there was no proportional increase in revenue. So, traffic was disconnected from their primary growth goal.

To course correct, they shifted to a metric of qualified leads—specifically, how many e-commerce customers they were converting when they visited their site. Now the content team is responsible for qualified signups, which means every test is aimed squarely at influencing this number. In short, their success is a combination of continual testing of growth ideas and tailoring all content and activities to a target customer.

Noah's team is driven by results alone. No big long-term plans, and no grand theories. Noah explains:

I don't think I'm a great marketer—and I don't even know if I'm that great at running businesses. I think what I've actually done well is find products that I just love. Then it's my responsibility to tell the right people in the world about it. That's what I do in marketing; I'm not a genius marketer or anything. I just think, 'Oh, that's a cool product. Oh, that person probably needs to know about it. Now, let me do whatever it takes to make that happen.'

I think for other people out there who want to improve their business or marketing acumen, the easiest thing, besides finding a product you love, is to go help people one by one. It's a common misconception I've seen in marketing and in businesses where people think: 'I gotta scale! And I'm gonna spin up all these Facebook ads! And I gotta try to figure out

Reddit! Or I gotta do content or PR,' or some other thing.

If you come back and just go one by one, either do live chats, do phone calls, do in person, do a manual service, I think that really helps you understand your customers better, and helps you understand your business better. Long term that'll help you do really well.

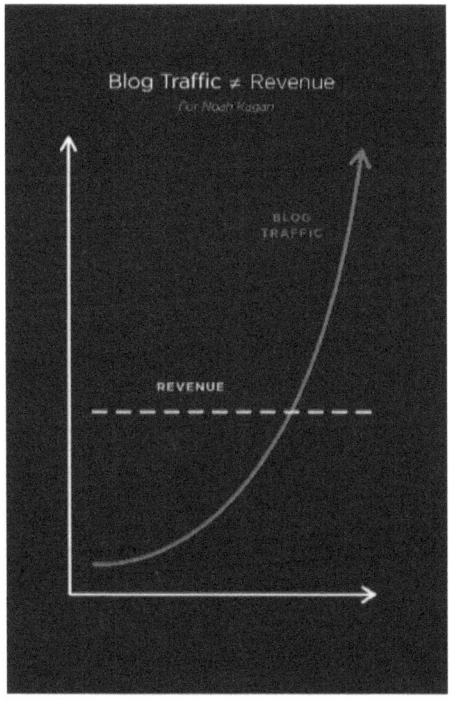

Figure 5.

Noah doesn't claim to know tons about marketing. He doesn't need to, because he knows how to experiment and shift his thinking to follow the results. That's content hacking. And his team exhibits these same traits. They're willing to take risks and then use their reverts when necessary—even if that means using them for 86 percent of their tests.

Three Content Hacks in the Wild

Without a doubt, real-world examples like Noah's are the best way to cement principles into your marketing. So, let's look at three more real-world content hacks. Now, just like everything else so far, they're not intended as a content-marketing buffet for you to choose from. After all, they've already been done. But they are pieces of world-class inspiration you can use to understand the content hacking mindset.

A unique new Business

April 05,2014

Figure 6.

Chapter 3
Creating the Right Content

"Prospecting – find the man with the problem."

– Ben Friedman

At CoSchedule, we recently launched a feature called Marketing Projects. It helps teams manage marketing campaigns. It's a perfect way to drive leads and conversions for our product. However, we use the content core to create valuable content around the core topic.

To do this, we used some good old-fashioned audience research to find two things:

A topic they're highly interested in

An angle that matches their needs

Now, I love tools—after all, our product is a tool. But when it comes to research, I never get too fancy. What I want, and what you should want, too, is to talk directly to your customers. And I think some of the best ways to do this are Google, Facebook, and LinkedIn user groups; email surveys; and simply picking up the phone and making some calls.

What you're looking for are conversations and subtopics around the main topic you'll be covering. In our case, we used Google to research similar content, plus we talked with our customers about their struggles and problems around our new feature. With both tactics, our primary goal was to hear how they described their problems.

First, we found popular blog posts and articles on marketing-project–

related topics. Then, we scrolled down to the comments section for each one. Here, we were able to read verbatim questions and comments from people in our target audience. This helped us pick up on the exact phrases they use that were related to our feature, while at the same time helping us more deeply understand their problems and gaps for which there wasn't a current solution.

Second, we talked to our customers. Loaded with the conversational ammo from our initial research, we dug even further into the struggles our current customers faced. We learned they were looking for four primary things:

They needed ways to "organize everything in one place."

They wanted a "marketing schedule template."

They needed help with "marketing campaign planning."

They had gaps in "marketing project management."

From this stage, we were able to tailor our feature launch to these problems perfectly. And we did so with content that fits perfectly into our content core. Not only did we know our audience was interested in the topic; we knew exactly how they explained their needs. And because it was a brand new CoSchedule feature, the angles we chose for our content intersected directly with our business interests.

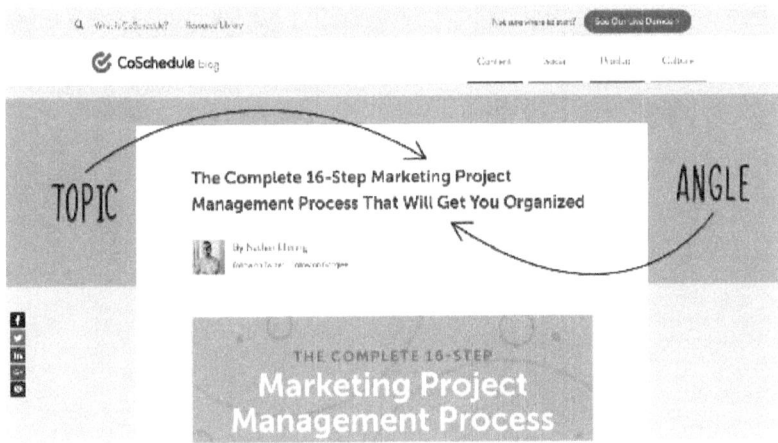

Figure 7.

The promise baked into the headline gives the reader the exact benefit as the feature itself. It's also an extremely useful post, clocking in at over 2,500 words, plus free templates to manage and organize marketing projects. And because that value is matched exactly with our feature's value, it converts traffic very well.

Finally, we included a single, clear, and compelling CTA. Here is the in-line body copy and companion graphic:

Figure 8.

Define Your 10x Workflows

Your 10x workflows will embody three characteristics. They will: be pre-approved, be lean, and include high standards of performance. Because they're pre-approved, they will reduce rework and needless hang-ups, getting the green light from your boss. Because they're lean, they will include only the essential tasks while being clearly and efficiently organized. And lastly, because they include a high standard of performance, quality won't suffer even though you're able to execute quickly.

When you create your workflows according to the following steps, you will be able to showcase a smartly organized process that will streamline productivity and get consistent results. You'll decrease the friction added by post-work approval processes because you will also limit the number of people involved. The fewer people weighing in on every detail, the faster work ships.

Just like the Oakland A's, your workflows will produce base hit after base hit. Your score will rise steadily inning after inning. Through the relentless execution of the fundamentals, what used to take you seven weeks—or even seven months—can now take just seven days.

Step One: Get Your 10x Workflows Pre-Approved

To start, imagine this scenario: Nathan Ellering, CoSchedule's head of demand generation, found himself in at a former corporate job. He was the manager of their in-house marketing team and invested heavily in content—or, at least he tried to. One of Nathan's main channels was the company blog, which ran on a daily publishing schedule.

This can be a grueling frequency for any marketer to keep up. However, difficulty was compounded by a messy workflow that looked like this:

Get post idea from a subject matter expert (SME)

Assign post to one of the writers

Receive draft from writer

Submit draft to SME for review

Address SME's notes and revise

Re-submit to SME for approval

Receive approval from SME

Submit SME-approved draft to the vice president of marketing for his review

Receive approval (or revisions) from VP

If revisions, edit draft again and re-submit to VP

If no revisions, submit to design

Publish post

Figure 9.

That's twelve steps involving five people, four levels of bureaucracy, and three layers of approval for each blog post. This meant approvals accounted for 58.3 percent of the total process. That's a lot of approving going on for one blog post.

Instead of being created with a bias toward shipping, testing, and getting results, it was bloated with unnecessary approvals solely in place as a check-your-ass measure. This bureaucratic process existed because one time, someone did something wrong—and this cascaded into wrapping an entire process around failure avoidance. Unnecessary approvals are a poison pill to culture and become huge obstacles to getting the marketing results you were hired to achieve.

If approval-laden processes like the one above sound familiar to you, good news is coming your way: 10x workflows solve this problem immediately. Nathan worked to restructure and fix this process following Step One. The key to streamlining is to reframe expectations. Instead of completing work and then submitting it for approval when completed, you will organize and gain approval on your workflows. Here's the process:

Create the 10x workflow.

Approve the 10x workflow.

Work the 10x workflow.

You will approve the workflow rather than making approval part of the workflow. When approval is part of the process, it becomes the enemy of shipping work quickly. Once you pass things up the ladder, approval will take forever. And you'll be buried in small, 10 percent tweaks because everyone who has a hand in the pie-making process wants to ensure their thumbprints are visible. After all, who wants to submit something to their boss—or their boss's boss—without looking like they've done some work?

If you get your workflows pre-approved, you'll ship faster. In turn, you'll get to 10x results in a fraction of the time. To create your 10x workflows, understand that the simplest approach is the best place to start. Your goal will be to pare down each workflow into its essential components. This process will do exactly that if you follow it closely.

Figure 10.

Here, you will wield the power of batching similar tasks together. In turn, this increases team member productivity by paring down the workload and enhancing focus. However, not only will your team be more productive, they'll be able to move faster than ever. Speed is the result of productivity, and that is what we are after.

As 10x marketers, we are looking to do more with less. If every blog post we publish helps us grow our email list, why not try to find a way to publish twice as much? Or at a minimum, keep the same publishing schedule and ship additional 10x projects? Content hacking, 90 percent good, and the 10x calendar are each dependent on you not only getting things done but doing them so fast your competitors freak.

As you increase your output, 10x workflows will also serve to reduce switching costs. This matters because not only does frequent task switching crunch productivity by 40 percent, but it also increases errors. Efficiency is both performing work quickly and doing work well the first time. Thus, you avoid reworking.

According to a 2005 study in the construction industry, rework can add between 7.25 and 12 percent to the direct cost of an entire project. Even if you don't have high overhead costs, your team's time is still worth a great deal—not to mention the project deadlines put at risk. In all, lean workflows will compound their value each time they're performed.

In addition, ensure your tasks are written with a definition of what "done" looks like. This final point of clarity removes ambiguity, reduces back-and-forth, and lets your team know exactly when they're finished. For example, rather than "Write headline and post," the task is labeled, "Write 20–30 headlines + body + proofread." Now the person executing the task understands exactly what the finished product of the task will look like.

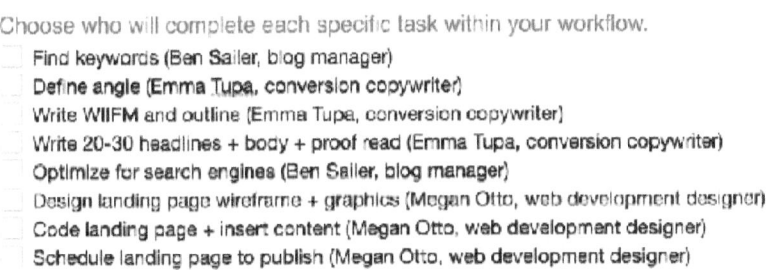

Figure 11.

Determine When Each Task Should Be Done

Generally speaking, most marketers run their content through the process, and once it is done, schedule it for publish. The problem is, this leaves a lot of room for thrashing during that all-too-common 10 percent push. Instead, adopting the content hacker mindset means picking a drop-dead publish date and working backward. Then, execute against that timeline and repeat for every post going forward.

This is what the exercise looks like when applied to CoSchedule's landing page example:

Determine how many days before publish each task must be completed.
- Find keywords (Ben Sailer, blog manager)
  - 18 days before publish
- Define angle (Emma Tupa, conversion copywriter)
  - 17 days before publish
- Write WIIFM and outline (Emma Tupa, conversion copywriter)
  - 17 days before publish
- Write 20-30 headlines + body + proof read (Emma Tupa, conversion copywriter)
  - 16 days before publish
- Optimize for search engines (Ben Sailer, blog manager)
  - 14 days before publish
- Design landing page wireframe + graphics (Megan Otto, web development designer)
  - 7 days before publish
- Code landing page + insert content (Megan Otto, web development designer)
  - 2 days before publish
- Schedule landing page to publish (Megan Otto, web development designer)
  - 1 day before publish

Figure 12.

For each task for which you create a 10x workflow, you'll notice an immediate bump in efficiency. And the fun part is, this is possible because you're eliminating redundancies and streamlining necessities. Now, who doesn't love doing less work and getting better results?

The goal here is for your team to produce more than ever before. This will happen because of the sweet synergy that happens when 10x workflows are combined with a 10x calendar. Your team will publish more focused content on a regular basis, giving you measurable results.

Estimate How Long Each Task Should Take

Next, we have a small, yet important step. Take a moment to set a limit on how long each task should take. When you do this, your team will understand the level of effort and time they should invest in each task. And, you're able to understand how long the entire workflow should take to accomplish.

Determine how long each task should take.

☐ Find keywords (Ben Sailer, blog manager) [30 minutes]
  • 18 days before publish
☐ Define angle (Emma Tupa, Conversion copywriter) [15 minutes]
  • 17 days before publish
☐ Write WIIFM and outline (Emma Tupa, Conversion copywriter) [60 minutes]
  • 17 days before publish

Figure 13.

These time limits remind me of a phrase used in agile software development regarding scope. Frequently, we will say a portion of a feature is "out of scope" when we are discussing a new development project. This means that before we start building anything, we make a decision about how much time we are willing to dedicate to the feature. The length of the timeline is based on the value the feature will provide the business.

So, if a feature will be only mildly useful to our customers, we may only budget one week for development. This means that our engineers will need to scope that feature to fit the timeline properly. Of course, we will forgo many "nice to have" elements by default, but the reality is that those things were unlikely to result in more value to the business, as we'd already measured the value in terms of one week.

The point is that time limits prevent thrashing, encourage shipping, and enforce the 90 percent good mentality. When you decide 10 percent projects don't matter, you need tight timelines to keep both yourself and your team in check. With this process, your team will immediately know when they are out of scope.

Step Three: Bake a Standard of Performance Directly into Your 10x Workflows

Finally, your workflows will be complete with a standard of performance to guide your team. A standard of performance is exactly what it sounds like - it's the quality and expected outcome of each workflow. This matters because it's a key facet of getting your workflow pre-approved.

The goal is for workflows to produce agreed-upon results. At CoSchedule, the standard of performance for each piece of content we publish is as follows:

Content Core: The topic must be aligned with our content core.

Keyword-driven: The content must be keyword driven for maximum traffic and long-term search performance.

Well-researched: Our content is thoroughly researched so it contains zero fluff and provides facts rather than opinions.

Comprehensive and actionable: The content will cover absolutely everything pertinent for our audience to know: what to do, how to do it, and how to get the results we promise.

Content upgrade: Every piece of content will have a custom content upgrade that will help our audience do what we're teaching them to do - they can access this in exchange for their email address.

Single, Clear CTA: Finally, every piece of content includes a single, clear, and compelling call-to-action—the content has a job to do, and the CTA is how we close the deal.

Marketers create content to produce results. Content is never the end goal; growth is. When you create your standard of performance, every person involved will understand the results your content (or any workflow you create) is executed to achieve.

In the next chapter, we're going to go deeper into our standards of performance for content. But it's paramount that whatever work you and your team are doing, you understand the results you're supposed to achieve.

Why Are Workflows 10x?

The core of 10x marketing doesn't equal haphazard and disorganized activity. Sometimes, this is the perception of the startup culture ethos. However, the 10x Marketing Formula is firmly rooted in this premise: people work faster, better, and more consistently by creating repeatable processes that consistently produce big results on a dime. This is all about focus and discipline.

In many ways, it's similar to the 10x ideas brainstorming process. There is a time for strategy and a time for creation. There is also a time to develop process strategy—affectionately dubbed 10x workflows. And by compartmentalizing these processes, you can create an efficient, 10x producing machine.

The relentless execution of the fundamentals, getting base hit after base hit, wins ball games. And more importantly, it wins championships, too. So, when you approach crafting your 10x workflows, just envision the Cubs' epic Game 7 World Series win. It was a 10x moment, and the same moments are waiting for you.

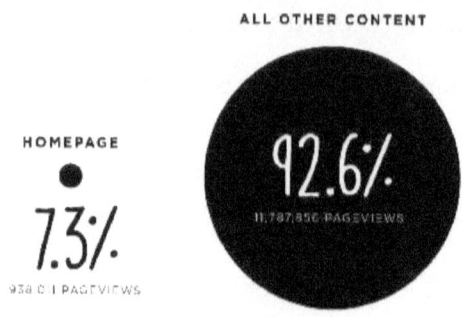

Figure 14.

We all say we aim to produce high-quality content, yet few of us actually write down what that means. If you simply become one of the few that write it down, you can stand out from the crowd. You need a way to execute higher quality, competition-free content, without having to go past the 90 percent good mark. All of this works together and is an absolute must.

Analyzing Content

Like Jeff, we analyzed our content to trace the patterns of which content drove results and which didn't. To do this, we looked at the last fifty blog posts we'd published. At the time, getting unique page views were the 10x metric we were optimizing for. So, out of those fifty posts, we read the top ten with the highest unique pageviews, and then read the bottom ten with the lowest unique pageviews.

As we did, it became quickly evident what qualities were reflected in these top performers. Because we compared them to each other, we found the qualities present in the best performers. And notably, those same qualities were either absent or underdeveloped in the ones that performed poorly. So, we planned posts based on these ideas, and they performed better than ever.

By developing our standards of performance based on data, rather than gut feelings, we consistently created high-performing content. This happened because we did the analysis and disciplined ourselves to stick to the standards. We decided we shouldn't publish something unless it was the best content in its category on the whole damn internet.

How to Create the Best Content on Any Topic on the Internet

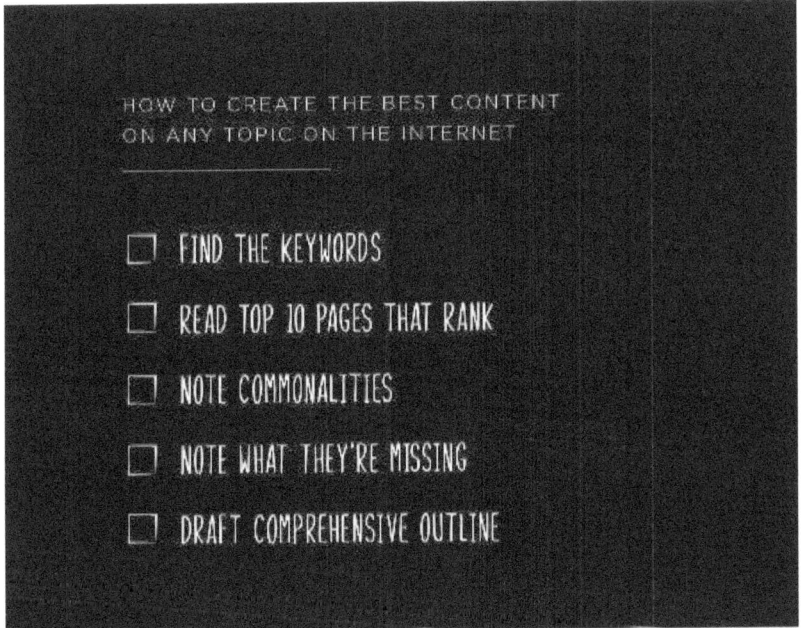

Figure 15.

Find the Keywords

Every piece of content we create is driven by strategic keyword research. This is because we want to optimize our content so our audience can find each piece when they need it most. However, our team goes further down the rabbit hole of Search Engine Optimization (SEO). We begin with a content core topic, then use tools like Moz (http://moz.com) and Ahrefs (http://ahrefs.com) to find a primary keyword or longtail phrase for it. We then outline three to five semantically related terms, which are simply terms closely related to your main keyword for which your content can also rank. Think of them as secondary keywords or phrases people may also search for when looking for content like the piece you're publishing.

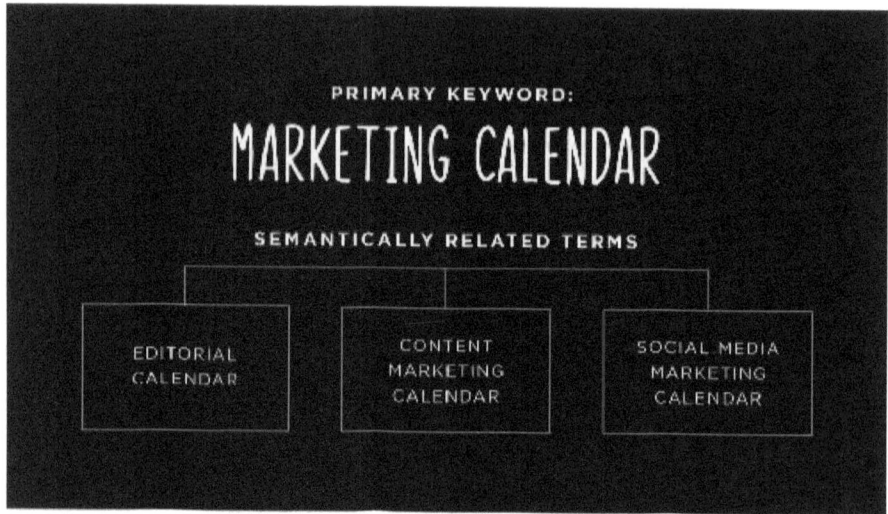

Figure 16.

You can find related terms with the keyword research tools I listed above. There is also an ever-evolving host of other tools to do the job. The bottom line is that your content can rank for way more than one keyword or phrase. And that's where semantically related terms come in. They amplify your content in search results for the long haul.

Read Top 10 Pages That Rank

Next, we search Google using our exact primary keyword. Then, we read, watch, or listen to every single piece ranking on page one. This means we study the top ten performing pieces.

Note Commonalities

As we study these pieces, we note the commonalities they share. This means we look at things like:

Content length

Content structure

Custom graphics and visuals

Social media engagement by platform

Content upgrades

Actionability and comprehensiveness

Tone of voice

Number of comments

Unique angles covered

Point of view and controversy

Data and research used

Note What They're Missing

This careful survey then allows us to note what the top-ranking pieces are missing. This is a vital step so we can create competition-free content. We don't want to waste time talking about the same angles in the same ways as everyone else. That's a red ocean; we want to swim in the blue ocean. With this step, here are a handful of things we can define:

Seek out a unique angle no one has talked about.

This is a perfect place to not only find competition-free content but also to assert a contrary perspective. Controversy is attractive and interesting. So, if we disagree with someone, we'll say so, and then prove precisely why our experience and data support our point of view.

Find ways to be more actionable.

This often means going beyond tips and into the territory of showing people exactly how to do what we're talking about. When you do similar research, you'll often find thin content that tells people what to do, but not how to do it. This is a fantastic way to set your content apart.

Identify gaps in visuals and graphics.

With even a quick pass, you can see how graphically intense your competition is. Are they just using the low-hanging fruit of a stock photo as a header graphic? Or have they invested in custom design, infographics, videos, GIFs, or other visual content? This helps our content creators and designers determine how to go beyond the top-ranking pieces.

Draft a comprehensive outline.

Last, we take all of the research we've gathered and focus it into a comprehensive outline. This outline defines five things:

The opening hook, along with two or three complementary CoSchedule pieces we're going to link to.

The content upgrade that will increase value, add actionability, and therefore be worthy of an email or trial signup.

The body content, with subheads, includes the main keyword and related terms, as well as custom images to be designed.

The supporting data and research we will use to prove our assertions.

The next step, or action, we will call our audience to take.

In all, this process ensures we create the best damn content on the internet every single time. It takes work—but it's worth it. Here's the deal. If it feels easy, it's not competition-free content. Why? Because it's been done before. These five pillars of content creation ensure we nail our content core and create competition-free content.

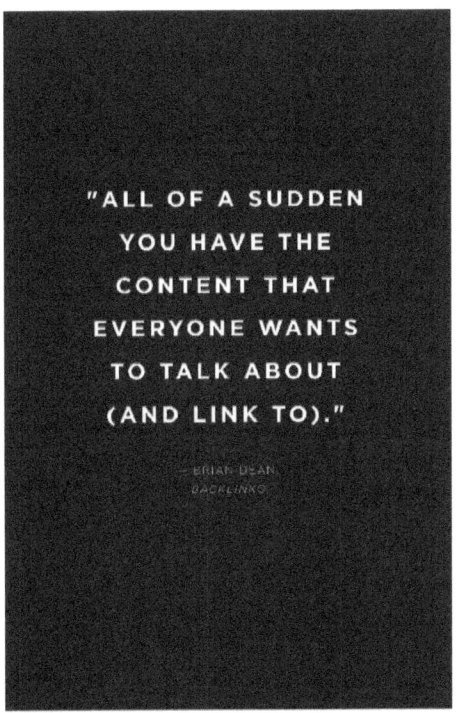

Figure 17.

10x Marketing Interview: Brian Dean and the Skyscraper Technique

As you can see, research plays a huge role in our content process. In fact, it's crucial to shipping 10x content every single week. But, you probably still have some questions. For instance, where should your ideas come from? If you've never had content produce big results for you, how do you figure out what has the greatest likelihood of short-circuiting the growth loop?

Whether you've experienced content marketing success or not, here's a simple, three-step hack that will work. It works so well, in fact, it's part of our own workflow. It's called the "Skyscraper Technique," and was developed by Brian Dean of Backlinko. Brian is a noted SEO authority and has used the technique to increase more than double his website traffic in less than two weeks after first putting it together.

Let's look at each step to put it to work in your 10x content.

Step One: Keyword Research

In Step One, you're really doing search engine optimization (SEO) work. You're finding the content core, competition-free topics you want to own in search. And even though the SEO landscape shifts continuously, the Skyscraper Technique focuses on this changeless factor: search will always begin with a keyword. Whether it's someone typing a phrase into a browser or using a voice search on their phone, this will necessarily hold true.

The goal of SEO research is obviously to find keywords your target customer is searching for. Overall, as Brian explains, keyword research that uncovers the intent behind people's searches is 75 percent of the game. To begin, brainstorm topics your target customer would search for when looking for information. Your keywords, or phrases, will fall into one of two categories: commercial keywords and informational keywords.

Commercial Keywords

Commercial keywords are the things your potential customers are searching for with credit card in hand. They're looking for a solution, and it's time to buy. For your company, these keywords will be closely tied to whatever you sell. However, they are often limited and highly competitive.

Informational Keywords

Second, there is a broader set of keywords called informational keywords. Researching these keywords is more nuanced. You must ask, "What are my customers searching for when they're not shopping for my product or service?" Then, list out all of the different topics they are searching for.

You can do this through customer conversations or even research on sites like Quora and Reddit. These keywords should be related to what you sell, but they don't have to be exact. For instance, if you were selling weight loss plans, your customer base is likely looking for things like workout routines and exercise equipment, as well. A perfect way to think about these things is as content core topics.

There are plenty of keyword research tools available to you, as well. There are too many to list or name here. But remember, if you can put a tool to work for you to save time and get better results, do it. A little research into the right SEO tools for you can go a long way.

Step Two: Analyze What's Ranking Now

After your research, it's time to analyze your competition. Simply read, watch, or consume every single piece of content that's currently ranking on the first page of Google for your chosen keyword. One of the mistakes Brian said he made early on was assuming if he created enough content, someday he would get more traffic from Google than everyone else—sort of like whoever has the biggest pile of content wins the game. However, he quickly realized that the path was futile. After all, every piece of content competes with hundreds of articles —including the ten top dogs on page one. It's a red ocean out there! So, if you create something that's even the tenth best on the internet, you're still not going to appear on page one of Google! It's not a volume game; it's a value game.

Step Three: 10x the Competition in the Face

Last, it's time to create content that's ten times better than the landscape you've just surveyed. One of the first articles Brian created using the Skyscraper Technique was about the roughly 200 ranking factors Google's algorithm used to rank web pages at the time. He knew the keyword phrase "Google ranking algorithm" was one he needed to own to become a leader in the SEO field.

So, he analyzed and read every top-ranking article for the keyword. And what he realized was that none of the articles had all of the ranking factors in one place. They may have had 50 percent of them—but not all. It was time to create his own piece of 10x content that added 20 levels plus a penthouse suite on top of the content skyscraper.

Brian created his content to be a one-stop shop for the topic. He made it as comprehensive as possible by curating every single published ranking factor. His resulting article provides an incredible experience for visitors. Because now, instead of having to track down the factors and cobble them all together themselves, they had it all right there in Brian's article.

There are endless ways to create content that's 10x better than the others. In this case, it was sheer comprehensiveness. Brian relates that he's also had success in 10x-ing design with detailed graphics, data-rich charts, infographics, companion videos, and real-life case studies.

This is a great opportunity to put a content scorecard to work, because, as Brian noted, "A common misstep is to overrate your own content, and underrate what's already on the first page." In the same way parents generally think their kids are the smartest and prettiest, our own content appears leagues better if we wear rose-colored glasses rather than look reality in the face.

Additionally, even if your content is better, it's truly a matter of degrees.

Think about your content like a product. If you launch a new and improved product, but it's only 5 percent better than current solutions, it won't be enough to galvanize people into switching teams and buying from you. Your content is the same way. You must create something that is 10 times better—the 10x principle at work. You must blow the existing content out of the water with comprehensiveness, actionability, design, and value.

The Anatomy of 10x Content

The reason we're putting such an emphasis on how to create 10x content is that everything you create has a job to do. It must have utility for your company and your audience. Over the years, we've had a variety of ultra-successful content pieces. We've also published a bunch of duds. To bring creating 10x content in for a landing, I'll drill further into our content standards of performance.

Topic

The topic is always aligned with our content core. It needs to be well chosen to help both our intended audience and our company. This means it directly intersects with the value our product adds and with our audience's needs. No parallel topics allowed.

Research

Data, examples, and experience fuel 10x content. And each helps us make sure the angle we target is backed up with facts while proving our advice will produce big results after practical application. One of our most successful articles ever is entitled "What 20 Studies Say About The Best Times To Post On Social Media." It clocks in at roughly 5,500 words, contains dozens of custom images and infographics, and goes uber deep into the science behind social media posting. And just like the title suggests, it presents findings from twenty different studies to prove what we're talking about.

Actionability

In our content, we never simply sprinkle a few bites of free advice people will struggle to put to work for them. Instead, we publish work that includes research-fueled advice coupled with actionable, step-by-step guidance, deep attention to detail, and a path to execution. The audience should be able to do exactly what we're talking about if they follow the process we provide.

Content upgrade

Closely related to Actionability is our use of content upgrades. They help people put our teaching to work. But they also exist to attract potential customers to use CoSchedule as their marketing calendar. So, we optimize everything to convert traffic into email subscribers who will continue to get this awesome, actionable content from us while also giving us the opportunity to share more information about the tool we offer that helps organize the chaos of content marketing.

Single CTA

To the end of content serving a business use, everything we do includes a single, clear call to action. We aren't trying to get our audience to do three or four different things on a page. We want them to do one thing, and we make that one action abundantly clear. Whether it's to sign up for our email list or trial our product, every piece of content has a clear next step for our audience to take.

We'll devote an entire chapter to CTAs and conversion psychology. But it's important to mention this here because revenue-generating action is the purpose of 10x content.

Graphics

Design has been a mainstay of our making our content competition-free from the beginning. We invest heavily in custom graphics in all our content, from blog posts to podcasts to webinars. As an example, we design between five and seven custom graphics for each piece. And, we design custom images for every social network, as well. High-caliber design immediately sets your content apart while also providing an opportunity to be useful to your audience. Visuals help reinforce and illustrate key concepts in our content.

Structure

The web is different from printed media. Blogs aren't books, and microsites aren't magazines, so, you need to write differently for the web compared to other media. Our content uses a structure that employs frequent visual breaks:

We use short paragraphs that are rarely more than three sentences long.

We use callouts for quotes and takeaway statements.

We use lots of bulleted and numbered lists.

We use the Click-to-Tweet plugin so our audience can share impact statements with a simple click or tap.

And finally, we organize our content well with subheads to guide the reader through the content.

Structure, though seemingly simplistic, is a vital part of the user experience. This is especially true for people reading our content on mobile devices. These best practices ensure a seamless experience on any screen.

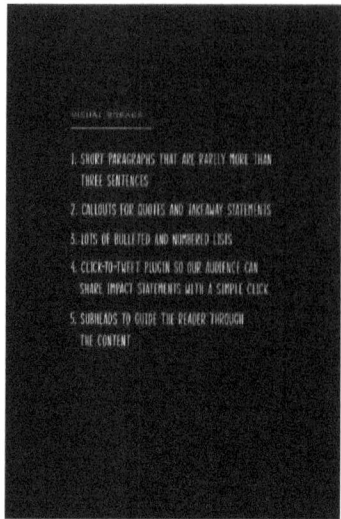

Figure 19.

How to Use a Content Scorecard

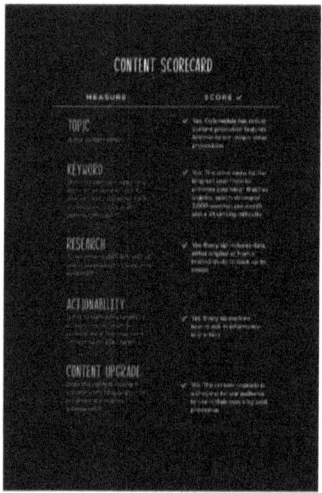

Figure 20.

* According to Ahrefs: "Traffic potential shows how much organic search traffic you can possibly get if you rank #1 for the Parent Topic keyword. We estimate this traffic potential by looking at the organic search traffic of the current #1 ranking result for that Parent topic keyword."

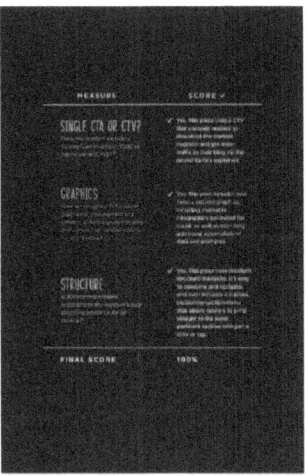

Figure 21.

* We will discuss CTAs and CTVs at length in Chapter 13, "Conversion Psychology." But for context, a CTA compels your audience to take immediate action, such as, "Sign Up Free Now—No Credit Card Required." A CTV compels your audience to enter the next stage of your marketing funnel by inviting them to value, such as, "Get More Traffic To Your Blog Posts Within 7 Days."

This blog post met every benchmark of our content scorecard. So, how did it perform? In its first thirty days alone, it generated 23,358 page views and 21 trial signups. In the following six months, it scored nearly 150,000 pageviews and is ranked solidly in the number one position on Google for its keyword. In fact, it's even captured the coveted "Featured Snippet," which Google explains this way:

How To Promote Your Blog With Social Media

1. Share your content in many places. ...
2. Include your blog link in your social media profiles. ...
3. Rock the power of 100 rule. ...
4. Clean up your open graph data. ...
5. Share your blog posts on social media right when you publish them. ...
6. Share your brand new posts more than once.

  More items...

How To Promote Your Blog With 107 Content Promotion Tactics
https://coschedule.com/blog/how-to-promote-your-blog/

Figure 22.

Google search for the term "how to promote your blog."

Creating Your Own Content Scorecard

Both Jeff Goins's content scorecard and ours at CoSchedule have proven invaluable. By holding your content to a high standard, you can also identify likely performance gaps before you publish. So, what about your content? Do you have a content scorecard that drives what you publish?

If not, now's the time to create one. Or heck, you can even swipe Jeff's or ours! Remember, statistically, your content is the functional homepage for your website. So, if your site is going to produce real business results, your content needs to meet the standards of performance to which you'd hold any other marketing effort. To create your own scorecard, start simply, and use this basic framework of questions:

What is our content's goal?

What characteristics are present in the content we've published that has accomplished this goal?

Is the topic within our content core?

Creating a content scorecard isn't enough, though. It also requires discipline to stick to it. Saying, "No, we won't publish this piece until it meets our criteria," is a big step. But you, and your team must commit yourselves to the practice if it's going to work. As with every part of the 10x Marketing Formula, the magic happens when you put it into practice. It's on you to make it happen. But when you do, you'll see results.

This Is Your Shot

This chapter could be summarized like this: create every piece of content with the assumption that it's your only shot at publishing the best piece of content ever produced on that topic. This will mandate well-researched 10x content that performs in line with your scorecard. It means creating stuff that wows your audience to capitalize on the halo effect, thus bestowing love on every new page visited, and even your product itself.

Every piece of content you create is your one shot to get results on your website. So, the primary question to ask when you start, and right before you publish, is this: "Will this content turn readers into customers by taking the next step in the process?"

Action is the measure of success—and creating a content scorecard is the place to begin.

Your 10x Toolbox

Put this chapter into action with your 10x Toolbox by visiting https://coschedule.com/10x-toolbox

10x Marketing Interview: Jeff Goins and the Content Scorecard

In this interview, author and speaker Jeff Goins explains how his team developed the content scorecard—a tool he says transformed their results.

You will have access to the full audio interview plus transcript.

[Template] 10x Content Scorecard

This template helps you score your content before it's ever published. It's a dead simple way for ensuring consistent quality and measuring potential impact before a piece is published.

10x Marketing Interview:

Brian Dean and the Skyscraper Technique

[Checklist] The Skyscraper Technique Checklist

This is a checklist for using Brian's "Skyscraper Technique" for content research and creation.

[Free Tool] Headline Analyzer

The Headline Analyzer is a free tool that will help you write headlines that drive traffic, shares, and search results. It is available absolutely free at: https://coschedule.com/headline-analyzer

Chapter 4
Who are you writing for?

"All progress takes place outside the comfort zone."

– Michael John Bobak

Imagine you're opening a restaurant.

You've found a nice place in the center of your home town next to a popular bar.

What do you do next? Design a trendy interior? Look for local suppliers? Go chat with the bar owner next door to do a co-promotion?

Let's say you start with creating your menu. How many starters do you need? How many main courses? And how many main courses should be vegetarian?

You start wondering—who will come to your restaurant? Will they prefer to eat meat, or fish, or vegetarian fare? And do they like a traditional menu or more adventurous dishes? Should the food be spicy or not?

Just like with a restaurant, you need to know who your blog readers are before you start writing. Readers have a choice of millions of blogs. Why will they choose to spend their precious time reading your blog posts?

If you don't know who you're writing for, your blog may go in myriad directions, and you end up speaking to no one. So how can you ensure your blog posts speak strongly to your target audience?

In this chapter, you learn:

- Why you should write your blog for one ideal reader only

- What to do if your blog targets more than one audience

- How to create your ideal reader profile

Why is the Strategy Behind Free Content So Important?

The problem isn't the Internet. It was the kind of subscribers they were attracting. Also, they were sending out the wrong kind of content. You can't just create content full of tips or even step-by-step guidance. There has to be something more. You have to make a personal connection with your audience. That means integrating with your own stories or even case studies from other clients. Think about a professional speaker or an author you admire. You've probably gained a lot of value from them, but I bet you it's not the step-by-step systems you remember most. It's the stories they tell. Every professional speaker knows the audience will forget their five tips before they even walk off the stage, but they remember the stories for years to come.

Your Strategic Myth includes your origin story, but it goes beyond this. It's a story about a dream. It's about overcoming challenges. It's about a hero who wouldn't take NO for an answer. There is a story inside you that you have to share with the world. And you're inviting them in along on your journey. You're inviting them to take part in your story and your mission.

There is already too much content online. You're not going to cut through all the noise online by publishing just another series of boring articles. You have to grab your prospects by the lapels and give them a story that will stick with them. It has to be memorable. It has to be entertaining. And it has to be something they want to share with others.

What story are you telling? Is it a story about just another business that wants a share of their hard-earned cash? Or is it an exciting story that inspires them?

By the end of this book, you will know who your ideal clients are. You will have a story to tell that they identify with. And you will know how to get your message out there using simple step-by-step methods that are proven to work in virtually every market.

Chapter 5
The Profile of a Copywriter

"The only limit to our realization of tomorrow will be our doubts of today."

– Franklin D. Roosevelt

If you have read so far, you may wonder (as I would do) why should you become a copywriter? How would you know you are fit for this kind of job?

Let me give you two reasons that convinced me a while ago:

- Even if it is one of the most competitive writing fields in the industry, is also one of the most lucrative;

- You find out if you have what it takes to be a great copywriter going through the following list. It is not necessarily a rule. The list puts together a personal point of view, but you will see that most of the professionals recommend the same.

Therefore, for successful content marketing you need:

To have a little bit of talent

I say a little bit because talent values too little if it is not accompanied by constant hard work. Talent in writing is not something that you have since you are a child. You discover it in time, and only after you have tried some samples. This part gets me to the second skill:

You love to write

I always believed that I was no good at writing, but I've loved writing since I've known myself. Therefore, if you love writing you most likely have a seed of talent in you. You will find some people that have talent and do not like to write, but this comes, from my point of view, as a natural hazard of the job.

Of course, you may have periods when you will be bored of writing, but this does not mean you cannot become a copywriter. I believe everybody experiences boredom from time to time. When you find yourself in such a period, take a short break, remember the reasons that drove you to (copy)writing and rediscover the passion in you.

I like to think that content marketing is like being in a long-term relationship with words. I do not give up; I just take it one step at a time and tackle difficult periods in a calm and relaxing manner. Talent, passion, and a lot of hard work will lead you to great jobs (and great amounts of money).

Be willing to start at low prices

I want you to understand that your job is worth the money, it's just that you need to be realistic! When you start as a beginner, you need to build up your portfolio to create a network. Until you get there, you should enter the market by having lower prices. I will tell you about how to charge for your work later on.

Be confident about being different

A copywriter can write for all sorts of businesses and in different areas. To become successful, you need to become an expert in only one field. Having a specialty increases credibility. Or, in other words, do not become a general writer. You discover the right niche for you by trying. Write copies for different niches. The ones that are easiest to do should be in the field that you will most likely become an expert in.

Be prepared to sell yourself

This part was the hardest for me. However, some sales skills will ease your way into earning 6 figures. Research how other people market themselves and find your own way. You can start a blog, in which you upload your portfolio (or samples), make your marketing strategy, and create a product around your services. At this point, do not be afraid of people who criticize you. Take their comments as feedback, and improve.

Be prepared to become a Nazi grammar

Be able to observe punctuation and grammar. Even if many people know a lot about writing and even love to do it, their content has grammar or punctuation errors. In content marketing, such errors are unacceptable. No problem at this point. However, you need to improve in this regard (if necessary) and double check the writing every time. The content is equally important to punctuation and proper grammar.

Develop Patience

In any new career, the beginning requires time and a lot of hard work. You will also deal with different clients, some more pleasant than others. Hence, you will need a lot of patience to deal with so-called "problematic" clients (I will detail below a short typology of "difficult" clients and how to deal with them).

A desire to speak up, with objectivity and humility

I put in here three qualities, that one needs to meet to be a successful copywriter. The part about speaking up is a must, as copywriters also express opinion/point of view. This is a harder aspect for shy individuals, but they can get away with it with practice (start speaking up in a group of close friends and with family).

The areas of objectivity and humility go hand in hand. The facts from your copy need to be analyzed as objectively as possible, so you offer the customer the closest point of view to reality. On top of this, no one likes misleading information.

As for humility, this will help you acknowledge your limits, and do your best with everything you know. Accept and use feedback. Never assume that you are too good. Even the best copywriters have things to improve on

Strategy and creativity

The easiest way to explain this: as your job as a copywriter requires you to address a specific audience; you need to create your content in such a way that you impress that audience. The two essential tools for this are: well-targeted strategy and a lot of creativity. Also, keep in mind that one does not go without the other.

Be available to write samples

In the beginning, when you do not have a portfolio yet, you will need to write samples to convince potential customers of your skills. Of course, you can use the best examples that you have already written in your "training" period. Keep in mind at this point (and every time you write something) to be original. Plagiarism is a definite no.

Be open to new opportunities

Having such a lucrative job, you may find new opportunities in places and within businesses you would have never expected. You will not be a beginner for the rest of your life, so, as you gain experience and your network expands, continue to search for better and more appealing projects.

Having all these, a copywriter will be able to:

Write/change a piece of content into a functional one;

I talk about functionality because the purpose of content marketing is, after all, to make content functional, to promote something, or to highlight an opinion. It has to have a high impact on readers. In a nutshell, a copywriter uses the skills of a writer and techniques of a copywriter to say something that captures audience attention.

Sell a product/service

This is the main functionality of content marketing content. Once the customer's attention is on the product, the words need to convince them to try that product. Hence, the piece of writing has to be both appealing and informative. The best copywriters (already) have the skills to focus solely on the main points that will determine whether the customer will buy the product/service.

Persuade the consumer

The end of each copy should contain what is called a "call to action". Therefore, after reading, each customer will (or not) be convinced to try, buy or promote the product/service advocated in the article/piece of writing. This requires from the copywriter, a high level of understanding of the readers and the target audience.

Use different styles of writing

Although many copywriters have a distinct way of writing, professional copywriters have the skills and ability to use different styles. The point is to be able to adapt the content to the target market language. For example, the language is different for children, adults working in big companies, or older people.

Create Solutions

A good ad is one that can answer a customer's problems. Customers look for products or services because they need that particular product or service in their lives. As a copywriter, it's your job to let these people know about how these certain products/services can make their lives easier and better.

Here are two things that you have to keep in mind:

- Define what the problem is. The "problem" refers to something that's missing in the customers' lives. For example, some may have the need for a brand-new perfume, cheap alternative medicine, the best dating website, or affordable flowers for a wedding among other things. Basically, every person out there has something that they need in their life. Target these needs and come up with a solution for it.

- Explain what you have to offer in a unique, catchy way. Lure the customers to you in such a way that other advertisers haven't done before. Be unique in creating solutions or copy. This is the only way you'll know if your copy can help your clients get the kind of profit that they want and if their services/products become popular, or at least, better known than they already are.

That's basically what you have to remember. Define the problem, come up with a solution, and voila! You'll be able to create a great copy.

Here are some examples of great copies that you can pattern your ads from:

Let's say your client asks you to create a public advisory as part of an anti-smoking campaign. Here's something that you can do:

"Want to learn more about lung cancer? Keep smoking."

This example is simple but very effective because it will hit people's minds in a way where they will easily make a connection between lung cancer and smoking. Thus, they will think that the more they smoke, the higher their chances of getting lung cancer are. It's as simple as that.

Next, if there's a product in the market that is gaining popularity, but the client wants it to be better known by more people or wants people to gain greater awareness about it, here's what you can do:

Let's say the product is a perfume.

"Haven't tried Fantasy by Britney Spears? Then you're surely missing out on something. It's great. It's powerful. It's fantasy."

Let people know that they are missing out on something because this will surely catch their attention. When people realize that they haven't tried something that others have already tried, then they will feel like they are not in the know, and thus, they will want to try that certain something right away. See? It's easy and effective.

You can also take a hint from classic Zippo ads. Zippos are lighters that are popular for their classic and stylish look as well as their longevity in the industry. One of the old Zippo ads bear the lines "Don't lose your Zippo. Lifetime friends are rare." This means that Zippos are a great investment because they can last for a really long time and they are truly reliable. Creating ads like this will surely boost your profits and your clients' profits as well.

Another tip would be to learn how to make sure that your text or copy on the image is used in the advertisement. There's a Duracell advertisement wherein a girl plays with a doll, and another older doll comes inside the house. The lines "Some toys last forever" are written next to the old doll. This refers to the fact that Duracell batteries are sturdy, reliable, and can last for a long time, which means that it would be good for anyone to buy them.

Humor is also very important. There's an ad for the restaurant 321 East that goes something like this: "How good is our steak? Last week, a man was choking on a piece and refused the Heimlich maneuver." Morbid as it may sound, this shows that someone was willing to die for a product that this restaurant is offering! Well, of course, this incident isn't true, but it can get people's attention and makes people curious as to how the steak tastes like. This is a very effective kind of copy.

Another great ad would be a one from Play-Doh. Beside the image of a can of Play-Doh, the line "Included: A lightsaber, a dinosaur, a rocket, transforming cars, toy soldiers, a spaceship, etc." are written. As you may well know by now, Play-Doh is a kind of clay modeling compound that's used to create different kinds of shapes and objects beyond your imagination. When kids see this, they will be more likely to bug their parents to buy them the said product, and thus, it proves to be an effective way of advertising.

Style Formatting

Make Your Content Visually Attractive

There are subtle aspects of content you must pay attention to:

The font

You must post your content in a font that is large enough and easy to read. As mentioned earlier, the internet has bred a generation of skimming readers with increasingly shorter attention spans. Clarity and visual communication such as attractive images help you retain them for longer on your site or copy.

Use short paragraphs

Internet content requires information that is carefully delivered in short paragraphs with each paragraph addressing a specific salient subject. Cramming too much information in a single paragraph does not help your writing in this generation of skimming and short attention spans.

Word Play

Writers have a natural tendency to want to play with words. Overplaying with words is fine when writing for writing's sake or for other literary goals. However, content marketing is about selling. If you are an English major and you happen to be reading this, you need to take a careful audit of the direction your writing is headed. Content marketing is salesmanship, not about wordsmithing. Content marketing needs you to arrest the reader's interest at the slightest opportunity.

Consequently, flowery styles such as those English majors learn in school will only usher your prospect out of the site without converting. This is the reason why choosing action verbs over flowery adjectives does it for content marketing. In fact, an efficient copywriter does not care too much about grammar if breaking it will deliver best. There is an interesting quip by one Gary Bencivenga, a proliferate blogger and writer, that a copywriter who shows off their writing prowess by playing with words is like a fisherman who shows off their hook.

Break the Rules

Observing convention is great. However, as a sales writer, you need to rediscover what makes a prospect tick. It is said that while on their colonization expeditions, imperialists in many places used religious approaches to get to their subjects. They appealed to the sense of security that religion offered. They appealed to what people needed. Religious values were palatable to the subjects; therefore, the imperialists ceased the chance to get their subjects to listen. The hidden agenda of expanding empires came much later after striking a chord with the locals.

Acceptability

Similarly, a good copywriter must understand the language of the customer, i.e. the readership. You must attune your writing to the needs of the prospect you have in mind. Consequently, you must use the names they use for what they want. This is the only way you are going to convince them that you don't preach water and drink wine. They will see you as one of them; that you understand them and that you know what they really need. The point here is to get the reader to feel you. Think in their language to you grasp their perspective. Only then will you identify a clear meeting point. Grammar nuance isn't going to persuade your prospect but the touch and persuasion coupled of course with the actual value they perceive you add to their lives.

Chapter 6
Clients Want Proven Results

"The harder the conflict, the more glorious the triumph."

– Thomas Paine

When it comes to content marketing, clients want proven results. They don't want to hire someone who may have simply written a few articles in the past and then hopefully will be able to put together a whole campaign to sell a product. They want someone who has experience, someone who has done this work before, can prove that the work was successful, and show that these clients are willing to pay a premium to get this.

Most clients understand that they are going to get what they pay for. If they are going to spend money on this campaign, and they want to make money on their product, they understand that they need to pick out a copywriter who knows what they are doing and can bring in results. The client would rather pay a little bit more to get the good results the first time rather than paying someone new to do the work, wasting time and money, and then having to pay the professional to come in and clean up the mess.

You will find that good clients know how much you are worth. If you are working with a client that wants to pay a low rate, there are a few things that are going on here. First, the client is either not aware of the current rate for a good copywriter and is just guessing at how much they will need to pay for the work to get done. Another issue could be that they are having issues with their cash flow and they are hoping for a miracle to happen, such as a good content marketing offering to do the services for a great price so they can get their business back up and running. And in other cases, the client is just trying to get work for free - they don't really care how hard you work, as long as they get the results that they want for a way below market value amount.

No matter the reason for the lower amount offered on a job, you don't want to work with any of these clients. The first client doesn't know your true value and may be difficult to work within the long term. Now you can talk to them about the price and some will realize that they need to pay more and will be happy to do it, but others will still want to get the discounted price because that is all they want to pay and they think the work is "easy enough for anyone to do." You don't want to work for these people because they won't value your work and you will spend way too much time making very little money.

For the second group of clients, you need to be careful. There is usually a reason that they are short on cash or have cash flow issues, and often this means that they are about to fail. You are not only going to miss out on some of the good income that you should be making, but the company is likely going to fail and you won't make a good income at all from them.

And finally, no one wants to work with someone who purposely puts the value too low. Many times, these clients disappear and never even pay, leaving you with a lot of wasted time and no money to show for it. Even if the client does end up paying you for the work that you do, you will find that they are really difficult to work with, will request way too many changes, and you will spend more time than it is worth to get the work done.

Finding the clients who will pay the rates that you deserve is critical. This is going to help out in a number of ways. First, they are going to value your time. Perhaps these clients have worked with some bad copywriters in the past and they are willing to pay more to get the results that they want, or they know the market value for what they want. Once you prove that you are the person they want to work with, you are going to be able to get those well-paying jobs that are going to make your income go through the roof.

But before you can work for these better prices, you need to make sure that you are able to produce those results. There are plenty of clients that will pay attractive rates but are not going to pay those rates to just anyone. You will need to have a method to show how you have been successful with these kinds of campaigns in the past. You will need to show some of the work that you have done with content marketing in the past, and if you have some numbers in place to show how successful they were, you will be able to impress the clients even more.

As a good copywriter, you should be able to show that you are going to bring in results for the client. A good client is willing to pay some of the higher rates, but you do need to make it worth their time. These clients are going to pay for the results, not just for your time to create the work. If there aren't any results, you are going to have some issues getting the income that you want.

The Power of Landing Pages

In the digital marketing and online business community, landing pages are crucial. They're the difference between a successful campaign and one that makes you question the results people claim to be getting.

The wrong ones will make the internet spew hate and vitriol then push you into a downward spiral leading to a long, slow, agonizing death.

The right landing pages turn browsers to fans, haters to friends, and customers to advocates. People share them on social media and the world creates hashtags in your honor.

There's a fine line between high performing landing pages and the ones that'll make you wonder if the time you spent on them was worth it.

Old advice like "use red in your headlines" and "create multiple columns on your pages" will kill conversions faster than a prize-winning thanksgiving turkey gets slaughtered.

Your audience is jaded.

They've been on the web for years. Many of them were born into the web and may know more about it than you.

You're doing yourself, your brand, and your customers a disservice by trying to get away with poorly designed and researched landing pages.

Why?

Because I know how powerful they are when used correctly. It's even more pronounced when you don't have much traffic. If your website is receiving a million visitors a month, you can disregard this book because you'll get customers and subscribers no matter what you do.

If you're like the rest of us mortals, then keep reading. You'll find gems in this book and learn how to create more powerful landing pages that move your business forward.

Before we dive into making the ultimate landing pages, you and I need to be on the same page.

A visitor can "land" on any page.

While those pages can and should be optimized for conversions (especially the about page, as it is one of the top three visited pages on a website), they're not what I'm referring to when I say landing page.

Whenever you see "landing pages" in this book, it refers to dedicated pages made and optimized to do one thing:

That could be to make a sale.

That could be to promote a sign up for a mailing list.

It could also be to promote a giveaway.

Whatever.

The overarching theme with the landing pages I discuss is they have one desired outcome. The rest of the pages on your website have too many distractions. Those include links in the body text, menu buttons, popups, footer links, a sidebar, etc.

Let's redefine landing pages to reflect the focus of this book.

Landing pages are standalone web pages distinct from your main website that has been designed for a single focused objective. This means your landing page shouldn't have global navigation, in-text links, or extraneous elements like a sidebar.

There are many types of landing pages.

1. Click through pages. These are pages, generally on e-commerce websites, used to promote clicking through to the next page where the sale can be made. Think of them as teaser pages which warm up the prospect for the main offer.

2. Lead generating pages. This is the most common type of landing page. Their focus is to get your visitor to part with their contact information so you can market to them later in a more controlled setting EG Email.

It's done by giving away something of value in exchange for the contact information. A few examples of lead magnets are:

- E-books

- Webinars

- Cheat sheets

- Video tutorials

- First chapter of a book

- Free consultations

- Contests

- Free trial

- Notifications on updates

- Whitepaper

3. Sales pages. The most important pages on your website. This is where the money is made and, by nature, has the lowest conversion rate. On average, e-commerce sites see a 2%-4% conversion rate, and SaaS companies see 3%-5% conversions.

Of course, your product or service could be a necessity, novelty, or other –ty that makes it convert much higher.

What kind of assumptions, you ask?

Well, for starters, you assume your headline is good. You assume your button placement is the best. You assume your offer resonates with your customers. You assume your copy is well written. You assume these and dozens of other things.

Those assumptions should be tested at every turn by data. You observe and react to the data. It doesn't matter what your gut says if the data doesn't back it up.

At times, the process can be tedious and discouraging. I want to let you know the tangible benefits you'll receive as a result of an optimized landing page. Look back at this list when you get tired of the optimization process and want to throw in the towel.

It'll always be worth it.

Benefits of Landing Pages

I'm only going to touch on a few of the many benefits of landing pages. There are so many, I could write a book solely on this.

I digress.

The versatility of landing pages is what makes them so powerful. You can change colors, fonts, images, copy, and anything else you want with just a few keystrokes and button clicks.

Try doing that with the design you paid your developer for. Or what about the marketing videos you're thinking about making. How hard will those be to change?

Anyway, let's move into the most powerful positives of landing pages.

Skyrocket Website Conversions

What if you had a three-page website? One page is your homepage. The other page is your about page. The last page is a landing page optimized for sales. You may convert at a few percentage points. More likely, you'll convert at below a percentage point.

What happens when you have dozens of landing pages in addition to the three pages I just mentioned?

You have one for giving away an e-book, you have another one for a nice tool, another one gives away a piece of software. Oh, I forgot the one you have for a free consultation. Together, the dozens of landing pages bring more than 10x your subscriber conversion rate.

Every subscriber you gain is another opportunity for a sale. With email marketing, you'll blow your normal conversion rate out of the water.

This isn't a book on email marketing, but the two go hand in hand. The increased conversions via landing pages, coupled with a strong email marketing campaign will do wonders for your bottom line.

Data gathering and usage behavior

It's the internet. We're all connected. Whether that's good for us as individuals is up for debate. There's no denying its good news for your business.

Imagine you're getting poor conversions on your product pages. You drill down into the data and realize most of your visitors are using Chrome and Safari browsers. You also notice you're getting much better conversion rates from visitors using Firefox and Internet Explorer.

You could ignore it, but you dive deeper and realize the difference is statistically significant (that means it's not a fluke).

You use an Android device and Mozilla Firefox when you access your pages. You've not experienced any issues when browsing.

You forget about it and start doing something else. While you're working, you can't shake the feeling that something's wrong. You can't ignore what you saw, so you borrow your friends iPhone and navigate to your landing page.

The images aren't lining up well, the text is off center, and the page looks like it was dug up from the nineties.

You're stunned.

You download Google Chrome and navigate to the page. The same thing happens. Elements aren't where they're supposed to be, your font colors are off, and it looks like a child put the page together.

You're mortified.

How many people saw this page and decided your business sucked? After all, what kind of company can't even put a page together correctly?

You figured out an important piece of information with just one data point. Imagine what you can do when you have multiple data points to compare.

Sure, Google analytics gives you information, but dedicated landing page software gives you the data you need without having to prepare tedious custom reports. I've been there; it's not fun or easy.

This is a more extreme example, but when you have accurate data to work with, you'll begin to understand gaps and see patterns you can exploit.

Better Data Backed Decisions

With better data come better decisions. I talked about the ability to gather data at the last point. Now, I want to talk about what you can do with that data. In business, you need to know your costs and the effectiveness of your distribution channels, right?

If a direct mail piece is pulling $500 in profit for every one-hundred spent, you'll ramp it up – right?

The same applies to the web. If your Facebook ad campaign is pulling in profits then you'll put more money behind it.

Of course.

With the vast amount of data you'll be able to collect, like where people came from, which ones became customers, which traffic source bounced, how long they stayed on the page, etc. you'll make better decisions.

How would you change your campaigns if you realized the thousand dollars you spent on Facebook was only bringing in half as much as the thousand you spend on Instagram?

I bet you'd cut your Facebook ad spend and refocus it on Instagram.

Your decisions cease to be made based on how you feel. They become decisions you're confident in. It's no longer "we do it like this because it's always been done like this" to "we do it like this because we've run the tests."

You make better decisions when you have better data. Hold your data inviolate.

Build Hype and Validate Products/Ideas

How do you think people feel about your product or service? Unless it's a matter of life or death, it'll get old.

When Facebook appeared on the scene, it didn't have one-tenth of the bells and whistles it does now. It was a place to catch up with friends and follow companies you like. Now, there are ads everywhere, you keep getting requests to play games, and it tracks your movements in the real world.

It's a bit creepy.

Even though we criticize the way Facebook has changed, it wouldn't be here today if it would've stayed the same.

No matter what you're doing or selling, you need to create variety in your business.

If you've had only a few products, landing pages are a way to introduce new products gradually while testing market feedback.

If your blog is playful and laid back, landing pages are an outlet to get down to serious business. It's your choice how you introduce variety. Landing pages just happen to be an amazing vehicle for it.

Cater to more User Segments

This follows on the heels of variety. You may have one or only a few products and not need anymore. Even if that's the case, your customers will use your product differently.

Take Pinterest for example.

The main website was built for a certain demographic of people. Those are well to do, educated, and married women. In 2017, men have become the largest growing segment of their user base.

Those are for the users — the buyers. They have another section of their website entirely for advertisers and business owners. These people are the ones who are paying the bills and need resources and tools to make the most out of Pinterest.

It's not limited to marketplace type businesses or social media. Think about a photographer. They take pictures at weddings, birthdays, bar mitzvahs, and everything in between. When someone lands on their website, they want information relating to their specific situation. They don't want the generic spiel.

You can apply the same principle to almost any industry. The financial services sector needs different faces for students, young workers, high net worth individuals, and businesses.

The construction industry builds retail spaces, homes, and multi-unit housing complexes. Do you think those people need the same information? No, they don't. They need content, images, and offers related to their specific situation.

Even if you don't have dozens of products, you have different user segments which have different needs. The more optimized landing pages you have, the more opportunities there are to connect with different market segments.

Improve Marketing Campaigns

One of my biggest pet peeves is clicking on a link for a specific item and being dumped on the homepage. Yes, the homepage may have some of the information I'm looking for, but I have to keep clicking to get the entire story.

Why?

Why would you make me do extra work? Every extra step I have to take is an added layer of resistance. Unless I'm a highly motivated buyer, I'm likely to bounce and never return.

The good news is that most websites are waking up and sending individuals to specific landing pages: not all, but most.

Landing pages improve marketing campaigns because you're able to drill down into the needs of a specific group of people. It can be a campaign which deals with your new vacuum cleaner, but there are different types of people who need it.

You have the single mom, you have the college student, and you have the elderly couple.

For each of these groups, you'll highlight different benefits to the potential customer. For the single mom, it could be how affordable and durable it is. For the elderly couple, you can touch on how quiet and easy to use it is. You can lead with low maintenance and its chic design when talking to college students (and how cheap it is).

Every marketing campaign and segment within that campaign should have a dedicated landing page. I know that's not always possible for various reasons. Chief of which is data and time, but it's something to strive for when optimizing your pages.

Put List Building on Steroids

This is the most popular use of your landing pages. It's almost as important as using them for sales pages.

Almost.

The sidebar on your website works, but many people experience blindness. Think about how you personally use websites. Do you give the sidebar more than a passing glance?

No?

Neither does the rest of the world. Most websites don't make it worth your time. They add ugly graphics, uglier opt-in forms, and the occasional greatest hits collection. < what does this mean in context?

On average, the sidebar conversion rate hovers between 0.5% and 1%. Those are good numbers. Most websites don't achieve that without rigorous testing.

Dedicated landing pages are a different beast. On average, conversion rates climb well into the teens. For every 100 people that visit a landing page created to get contact details, 15-20 of them will become email subscribers.

I'm sure you know as well as I do that email subscribers are the bread and butter of cost-effective marketing campaigns.

With an optimized landing page, those numbers can easily double or triple. It's not by accident. A landing page focuses the attention and gives your prospect two options.

Either they perform your desired action or they exit the page. There aren't a bunch of miscellaneous links for them to click on, no menu buttons, and only one call to action.

Improve Credibility

Last but not least, landing pages improve your credibility in the eyes of your visitors.

Let me explain.

Throughout your website, you have elements scattered about. Maybe you have featured logos on the about page and homepage.

You also have testimonials on different portions of your website. They work together to let the people visiting know you're credible. In addition to that, you have a great design and other things going for you.

With a landing page, you incorporate those elements into one page.

You have testimonials, featured logos, and a unique design all on one page. You use persuasive language and pull out the big guns to establish trust.

Instead of someone needing to navigate to the homepage, then the about page, then the testimonials page, and maybe a few blog posts, you do the work for them with a well-designed landing page. It's a shortcut to the credibility needed to make a sale.

In a nutshell, landing pages are an asset. The more you have, the greater your conversions across the board. In a 2016 study, it was discovered that conversions went up by 55% once a website had ten or more landing pages.

That means just one landing page won't cut it. Five landing pages won't cut it either. It's a constant process of creation and iteration. Throughout the rest of this book, you're going to be equipped with the insights and strategies to turn your landing pages into works of art.

Chapter 7
Content Marketing For
Facebook Marketing

"A successful man is one who can lay a firm foundation with the bricks that others throw at him."

– David Brinkley

In the content marketing industry itself, there are niches that you can also specialize in. One particular content marketing niche where demand for experts is increasing is social media.

Facebook is the undisputed champion of all social networking websites. Many websites have risen from obscurity by using Facebook alone as a marketing tool. Websites that struggled to gain traction when using search engine marketing are turning to Facebook marketing as an alternative solution.

Facebook Content Marketing

Facebook is successful because of its ability to retain people's attention. The features on a user's profile page and timeline are so engaging that many people tend to spend hours on these pages without being aware of it. Companies and smaller businesses take advantage of these features by making sure that their posts show in these pages.

To be an excellent Facebook copywriter, you should first be familiar of the common objectives of companies and business that are using this social network as a marketing tool. Here are the common goals of companies that market on Facebook:

- Product/company introduction

- Awareness

- Popularity

- Event promotion

- Increase online and offline sales

Before you can start marketing on Facebook, you should first identify the need of your clients in their marketing campaign. If they are not aware of their marketing goals yet, then help them establish their goals by interviewing them and analyzing their motives.

Helping reach their goals through content marketing

When content marketing for Facebook, you have your own tasks to help the clients achieve their marketing goals. First, you need to get the user's attention. Then, you need to retain their engagement. In other words, you need to keep them reading. Lastly, you need to make them take action.

On Facebook, a user can only perform a few actions that can benefit your client; these are liking, sharing, and clicking on links. If your copy has made the target users take favorable actions, then you have done your part as a copywriter.

Liking

A "like" is Facebook's version of an up-vote. It has two purposes. First, it increases the reach of a post. As people like your post, it may also be shown on their friends' newsfeeds. The posts that were liked by friends will show in either on your newsfeed or in your notifications box when you click on the bell in the upper right side of the newsfeed page.

The second function of a like is as a subscribe button for pages. The posts on a liked page will appear in the person's newsfeed. This will increase the probability that future posts will have better engagement because more people will see them.

Sharing

Sharing, on the other hand, is the feature that will make your posts become viral. When people share your content, it will appear in their timeline as well as in their friends' newsfeeds.

Clicking on links

If you promise your clients that you can make a lot of users click on their post links on Facebook, then you will have a considerable edge against your content marketing competitors. This task, however, is not easy to do because people don't easily click on links.

There are generally two ways to get clicks, likes, and shares: through organic Facebook marketing and paid advertisements. Your role as a copywriter is to increase the likelihood that people will like and share content in organic or paid marketing.

You can do this by following these tips:

Appeal to people's emotions

People on Facebook are there to have a good time. They spend so much time on Facebook because posts remind them of people they have met and things that they have experienced in the past. That is why posts for things like "Throwback Thursday" persist until now. To make them like or share a post of a page, you should use emotional topics in your copies.

Use your target user's language and way of speaking

When posting, you could appeal better to a specific market if you talk the way they do. If you are targeting engineers, for example, then you should also use jargon and technical terms that only they will understand. If you are targeting a specific nationality, you may become more successful if you post status updates and links that speak their language.

Use words popular on the internet

Some words are more magnetic to people on the internet than others. For instance, the word 'awesome' is a great word to use regularly if you are targeting users in their teens and early adulthood. Other magnetic words are: "Wow", "Never", "Inspiring", "Die or Dead", "Definitely", "Feel", "Terrified", and "Amazing." (seems like an odd list)

In the past, words like "Free", "Now", and "You" were eye-catchers but many internet users have now associated them to annoying ads and pop-ups. You should expect the same phenomenon to happen with any attention-grabbing words on Facebook. People will eventually learn to ignore them when they become too popular.

Use the "post description" to catch attention

The post or ad description is the first thing that users read after your page name. If that part is not interesting, then they will move on to the next item on their newsfeed. You should use this to gain attention and create curiosity by adding more powerful words. For instance, popular pages use "this", "that" and similar pronouns often. Here are some examples:

"This man can't believe what he was seeing"

"That's not right. This shouldn't be legal."

Adding a picture that matches the description will also increase the likelihood of a like, a share, or a click.

Use the power of the red arrow in photos.

One of the most effective combinations when making people click on links is by using the powerful pronouns suggested above and adding a photo that has a red arrow to refer to the thing or person being represented by the pronoun. For instance, if your headline goes something like this: (missing headline?)

You should also add a photo of a person driving while texting and an arrow pointing at the driver. This will not only grab the attention of the users but also make them curious as to what will happen to the driver.

Conclusion

"The competitor to be feared is one who never bothers about you at all, but goes on making his own business better all the time."

– Henry Ford

Despite the overview of this book, you must take it further if you want to become the best copywriter you can. Throughout the book, the tips that were given were to help you to see that content marketing isn't just about writing an elaborate description of a product. It's about convincing a target audience they can't live without having a certain product. It's about their belief in the product. It's also about being able to express all of this in such a way that your message targets the audience most likely to buy the product you are selling.

Look into the competition and find their weaknesses. The iPad advertisers did this perfectly, in that they knew the public still suspiciously views the innovative and complicated systems produced by iPad competitors. Instead of describing their system in a really complex manner, they demonstrated it as totally suitable to everyone's lifestyle in a stylish way. That is clever, honest content marketing and it hits the target audience in a way no one could have anticipated. The new iPad Air has equally taken the imagination of the public by storm by offering a lightweight the old iPad didn't offer. You'd be hard-pressed to make an iPad user part with the technology once you made the sale.

We told a similar story about cut-price airlines and how luxury airlines exploited the fact that "no frills" may not be what a discerning traveler is looking for. A good copywriter knows the following:

170

- The benefits of the product to target population

- The competition and what it offers in comparison with your product

- The medium by which advertising will be spread

- The time limits or constraints the copywriter must work within

- The public sector at which the adverts are aimed

Once you add the wonders of great vocabulary and come up with a brief but imaginative copy people automatically associate with the product, you will have sufficient information to persuade the public to buy your product. Look back at the catchphrases we shared with you, as some of these are extremely typical of what is being used to lure the public in these days. Some of these will last for generations as consumers believe in what they are investing.

You are selling a brand. Think Nike and the catchphrase that instantly comes to mind is, "Just Do It." If that doesn't push people who are having trouble making up their minds, then nothing will. Brands depend upon copywriters to come up with the right copy to sell, and the examples shown to you in this book are first-rate examples.

Disneyland is still selling tickets based on the fact that it's purported to be "the happiest place on Earth." This appeals to both grown-ups and kids alike, who are seeking out an adventure that takes them away from the doldrums of normalcy and into another world where people are all happy.

All of this is a lot for one person to work on, but it's all part and parcel of working as a copywriter. If you feel you have the imagination and can play with words to pass on a message, then perhaps this is the career for you. With a Bachelor's Degree in Advertising, followed by or during which freelance work is undertaken, you stand a good chance to become one of the best. Keep up to date with current trends, and you will find the work is rewarding as you experience success.

Freelance work is always available, though if you wish to have the security of being employed by an advertising company or a public relations company, this should be your goal. Online companies are offering jobs to copywriters, but be aware you may lose copyright of written work, as clients paying for work tend to take that as part of the deal. Mind you, that's not much different to working for an agency because the agency takes copyright on what their employees produce. If you are happy with that, you can think of this as being a practice run to actually working in an advertising environment with the agency taking all of the credit for the work you produce.

It's a very satisfying career and one that suits people who are not afraid of new things. It would also suit those who are open to changes and working for different clients with different needs. Specializing in a field is also possible, such as cosmetics, industry, etc., and your specialist area could also be backed up by qualifications that show your knowledge of the product range. However, never close the entrance door to opportunity. The best content marketing I ever did was on a product I knew nothing about before undergoing all of the investigation needed to be able to produce. The fact that the product was new to me opened up new avenues of exploration, and perhaps it was the freshness of approach that made it such a success.

I wish you well in content marketing. You may have decided by now content marketing isn't for you. You may not want your writing associated with branding or product sales, but for those who do, this is a rewarding career move that gives a steady flow of work and great pay. You may not earn millions, but you will never know until you try. It's enjoyable, for every job taken is different, and you change your approach every time you have a new copy to write. Otherwise, you get stale. If you are stuck in your ways as a writer, you can't expect to pitch like a pro, which is what content marketing is all about.

Content marketing takes your writing skills one step further than straight writing. Does that mean that you can't have heroes and heroines? Of course not. You only have to see the adverts on the television screen to know that even advertising copy allows you the benefit of creativity. Think of all the memorable advertisements you have ever seen and know that behind every one of them was a very clever copywriter who somehow got it right. If you can remember the advert, they did their job properly. That's what you need to be aiming for.

The adverts that stand out in your mind or the copy you read on the Internet that struck a chord with you is clever content marketing. This book has many exercises and you will be able to go through them time and time again, choosing different products and objects to use. It pays to work on items you find boring as well as those that you find exciting because a good copywriter can make even the mundane sound necessary and exciting to the buying public. If you have spare time, pick up an object and try to describe it using all of the styles relevant to content marketing - all of the practice you get helps you to be able to change styles instantly to suit the market and the age range to who you are aiming your copy. Often, bad content marketing shows up big time, which allows you to keep working within the parameters set by your client without making you look foolish or as if you have not understood the brief you have been given.

Bonus Material: Passive Income Ideas For 2020; A Step by Step Guide to Easy Passive Income Ideas For 2020 and Beyond

Are you ready to invest your money into creating passive income streams that inflate your monthly income? These are some of the hottest, proven methods that you can start with, today.

You're not going to get rich earning a salary. You need to take those savings and make money from money. But how? It can be harrowing and risky to invest in new income streams for the first time. The chance that you will lose money is high. That's why you need a guide just like this one.

In *Passive Income Ideas for 2019*, I detail some of the most lucrative methods of earning additional income available for the modern investor. I take a candid, unfiltered look at opportunities in social media, drop shipping, affiliate marketing and renting. There is real money to be made here!

In this ideas-guide you'll learn:

- Why passive income will get you where you want to go

- How drop-shipping works and how to get started selling

- What affiliate marketing is and how to make money this way

- How to invest as someone interested in passive income

- How to leverage social media for passive income generation

- About renting, website flipping, selling eBooks and being a creative

The sky is the limit when you're no longer a slave to your monthly paycheck. You'll lose some. And you'll win some too. After a while, you'll just keep winning. That's when your life changes.

Discover how to seriously create passive income streams that will free you from your current job. It's easier than you think, and all it takes is commitment and a sharp mind!

Learn how to get started with passive income in this guide.

Buy the guide, and start earning!

Introduction

Are you struggling to make money? Do you feel like you are spending most of your time, yet you have nothing to show for it? Do you admire those millionaires and billionaires on TV and wonder how they do it? If the answer is yes, then you might want to ask yourself how you can get out of your own way and start making more money. The answer is to that is also simple; you are not doing everything you can to make more money. You may wonder how that is if you are spending all your waking hours working. The answer is you do not have a PASSIVE INCOME stream. For years, rich people have understood that it's not how much work you do that makes you rich, that it is the quality of work that you do. You can spend all day working hard but still get paid minimum wages for it. There is also the danger of getting fired abruptly which makes you lose everything if you were not prepared.

Rich people understand that the money they have should work for them. They put their money in avenues that make them more money. They, however, do not sit down and enjoy their wealth. They keep putting their money in avenues that keep making a profit. They ensure that they make money even when they are not involved in said investments. This is what separates the rich and the poor.

If you have a little money and a lot of patience, then this is the book for you. Active income is the money you receive in your bank account that you earn from a job you do. It is what most people rely on to survive. For years, people have been urged to save money before they spend the rest. Even if your bills take up a huge percentage of your earnings, you can still save something. If you can't save anything, then that tells you that you are living beyond your means.

Don't put all of your money in a bank and assume that it is safe there. It might be safe, but it is not doing anything to safeguard your future. That money is what you should take out and invest in passive income generating ventures. Passive income is that which you earn even when you are not working for it. You get money from doing nothing basically. To earn a passive income, the bulk of the work is done upfront, and then the return will trickle in for as long as the investment remains active. The money you receive monthly may not be significant, but if you save it for a long time, together with compound interest, you will see the difference. You have to be patient before you see some tangible impact of your impact, but once it starts, it never stops.

There are many ways to make passive income and the returns from each vary. The more the return, the more you may have to get involved. I'm not saying you have to spend all your time on it. I'm saying you have to be involved. You may need to put in a little time to make the investment earn more, but it can still run without it. If you hate doing work, this is not for you. This is because passive income is not a get rich quick scheme. The work may be demanding, but the results make it all worthwhile.

The fact that passive income is a sure way of making extra money doesn't mean that the field remains rigid. You will constantly have to learn what is changing in the industry could make a world of difference in your returns in the long run. Look at trends and what people are looking for, but you still need to add our personality to it to make it even better.

Why the Need for Passive Income?

Even though we keep saying that passive income is money we don't have to work for, we have to remember that we traded that money for time sometime in the past. Passive income is a direct time of continuous efforts over some time. Even if you still earn from something you created ten years ago, there is no shame in telling that to people. There would be nothing unethical here especially if you did some work that is paying off years later.

- You will be free to pursue other things instead of chasing after money. You may still have your active income, but your days will be freer for you to rest and spend time with family instead of taking a second job to meet your basic requirements. Some people earn a lot of passive income that they can leave jobs they hate to pursue what they are passionate about. They are sorted even if their passions don't pay them right away.

- You will be able to plan for the future with the extra money. The greatest fear among working people is what will happen if they retired, and they are more worried if they are unable to put something aside for retirement when they can no longer work. Passive income eliminates that from your mind because as you work for your day to day expenses, your investments are working for your retirement.

- If you are trying to build multiple passive income streams, you can do so as opposed to traditional jobs here you are limited to a desk in a particular place. The internet becomes your workplace as you can communicate with clients and potential customers without leaving your home.

- With passive income, there is nowhere else to go but up if you play your cards right. This doesn't include risky investments. It includes the streams of passive income that have worked for many years. Even if the return starts out small, there is steady growth over a period of time as long as people are still interested in what you are selling. This will also happen if you keep marketing yourself and establishing yourself as an authority on a certain subject matter.

- Passive income is the foundation for wealth in the long run. The discipline it takes to work on something other than the one you have to do makes you appreciate the money you make. You may be a business owner that makes a lot of money. Until you make your money work for you aka investing, you are still not wealthy.

- Passive income saves you the most precious commodity that you can't gain back once lost–time. If you can exchange the time, you spend chasing money to pay bills and survive then you have won in life. As John Wooden so elegantly stated, "Don't let making a living prevent you from making a life."

Chapter 1: Dropshipping

The best time to plant a tree was 20 years ago. The second-best time to plant a tree is today.

-Chinese Proverb

Drop shipping has recently gained traction in the passive income space. It has especially been very profitable because of people's love for online shopping. Here, you as the seller have a website, but you don't necessarily own the product you are selling. It is like a brokerage between the customer and a third-party seller. You never see the product because the product is directly shipped from the third-party seller to the client. The third party here is a wholesaler or a manufacturer. You as a drop shipper never handle the inventory, therefore, reducing the need for a physical location as with usual retailers.

How Does Drop Shipping Work?

The first thing to notice is that Drop shipping is a service that is provided to a customer by a person behind a computer. The manufacturer produces items for sale but doesn't sell directly to the final consumer. This is because it rarely makes any financial sense to sell an item at a time if they deal with millions of products at a go. They offer their products at a lower price in bulk and have little to no purchase requirements, making it convenient for retailers with a lot of capital and wholesalers to buy directly from them. The wholesaler buys from the manufacturer and then raise the cost a little higher to make a profit. They also sell most of their products in bulk as opposed to a single item. The end consumer, therefore, can purchase items whatever the number from a retailer. The retailer buys from a wholesaler and raises the cost even higher to cater to their profit margins. These are the three groups of people that are available in a supply chain, and therefore as a drop shipper, you are a retailer. The drop shipping model is not visible to the end consumer at all. You as the drop shipper can purchase your products from any of the three groups even if you are a retailer. As long as any of them is willing to ship their products to your end user, they are "drop shipping" for you.

Step 1: Order Placement by Customer

A customer surfs through your niche website and finds a product that they want to buy. You as the merchant gets a message informing you of the purchase. Simultaneously, the customer receives a confirmation message of the purchase. The order is automatically generated by the software and sent via email to both parties. The payment is also automatically processed by a payment software, and confirmations are made to both parties.

Step 2: Order placement to the supplier

The order confirmation message is sent to the supplier so that they can process and ship the order to the customer. The supplier debits the total cost of the item from the merchant's account. Their price will be lower than what is charged by the merchant. The price will include order processing fees, shipping fees and the cost of the item. It is therefore up to the merchant to have considered this when they charged the consumer.

Step 3: Order Dispatch from the supplier warehouse

The supplier boxes and ships the item to customer depending on how fast their service is. All this should be included when marketing to the customer. The merchant's logo, address, and contact number are what shall appear on the box and not that of the supplier. Upon shipping, an alert is sent to the merchant along with a tracking number for the order. They also send an invoice for accounting purposes to the merchant.

Step 4: The merchant informs the customer about the shipment

An email alert is sent to the customer with the order tracking information by the merchant through the store's software. The order is complete at this point.

How to Find Suppliers to Work with

As I said before, the difference between success and failure in drop shipping is a reliable supplier. The end user doesn't know that there is a third party involved in the sale. Therefore you will be the one responsible if the item is not shipped, is damaged or of poor quality. Consequently, one needs to work with a supplier that will work well with your business model. You will also need to differentiate between legitimate wholesalers from posers and scammers. How can you separate the fake from the true wholesalers you may ask?

- They want you to pay them a monthly fee instead of charging you for the items you order from them. A legitimate supplier may charge a processing fee, but it is a reasonable amount, and they explain what they are charging you for so you know beforehand. Legitimate fees you will encounter are order processing fees that are added to each order you make. They will also have a minimum amount of goods you buy as your first purchase to weed out buyers from window shoppers. Instead of buying the items, you can advance them the total amount for an order that will go into your merchant account.

- If they are claiming to be wholesalers and yet they are selling directly to customers. This makes the prices go way up as they want to make as much money as they do if they sell directly to the client. That will eat into your profit margins.

There are many ways in which a merchant can find wholesale suppliers to work with.

1. Getting in touch with manufacturers

If you know the products you want to sell, looking for manufacturers to work with is not hard. All you have to do is finding out from them a list of their distributors. From then you can look for the one that does drop shipping and asks for requirements to set up an account with them.

2. Make use of the internet

The internet is full of information as everyone is advertising online. Depending on your niche, many people offer the service you need. Be careful as you can also encounter scammers. Don't just settle for the first suppliers that you see on the top page. Go deeper into the search engines as many good wholesalers may be hidden in the result searches. Look at the offers as opposed to the design of their websites. Don't give up on the first try and don't expect to get a good wholesaler immediately.

3. Scout, your competitor's supplier

Finding a wholesaler is hard and what better way to get one than good old fashion espionage. You can order from your competitor. You can call the number on the return address which is more likely to be the supplier.

4. Trade fairs and shows

Many manufacturers go to trade fairs where they network with potential retailers. The trade fairs are arranged according to the products, and you can easily pinpoint manufacturers in your niche. Some are free, and others have an attendance fee. Take advantage of many manufacturers in the same place.

5. Directories

There are many directories in the market that you can look for suppliers in your niche. They include SaleHoo, Doba, Wholesale Central and so on.

Attributes of a Good Supplier

- Professionalism and experience

If you are new at drop shipping, a professional representative will be able to talk you through the process and assure you along the way. They can also be able to answer your questions on any topic you may have.

- Around the clock support

Suppliers that answer the client's questions swiftly inspire confidence with the client.

- Tech-savvy organization

Because drop shipping is done from all corners of the globe, technology is the only thing that is unifying every player in the game. Orders and payments have to be done swiftly and securely through state-of-the-art software to improve customer experience. At the bare minimum, they should have email connectivity.

- Good location

If you are a drop shipper, you may want to look for a supplier that is close to almost all your clients to improve the delivery time while reducing shipping costs.

- Efficiency

A good supplier cares about your customer satisfaction which will guarantee you a repeat customer. They will provide good quality products and handle the shipping process with care and urgency.

How to Pick the Right Product for Dropshipping

Drop shipping is an online business, and the best way to know what people want is to search on the Internet. With SEO, it is easy to understand what people are looking to buy online through keyword searches. You can also see what people in your geographic location, what to buy and then what is in during a particular season. Remember that drop shipping is not a static business and those that evolve make the most money.

Consider the price at which the supplier is offering. The price at which you offer the customer should be reasonable; otherwise, you will need to offer phone support for assurance. The recommended price range for most online customers is $50-$200. Sell a product with a MAP (minimum advertised price) pricing so that there isn't much difference in prices between you and the competition.

Look at the scalability and longevity of your business. Your product should be able to stand the test of time and the tides of trends. Consider how you can market the product to potential customers. Sell things that go together so that the customer doesn't click away from your website. Sell items that do not change with time or perishable goods.

Look at what customers need to find the perfect items to sell. If something can be bought at a local store, then it is not worth the time. Avoid bigger and fragile products as they are expensive to ship and may break down during shipping. Also, avoid items that could be faulty when the customer tests it out. You want to run a business without returns and complaints to keep getting positive reviews.

Advantages of Dropshipping

1. Starting capital is small compared to having a physical location

All a merchant requires is a website to display the products they are selling. They do not need to buy any inventory or storage space to keep it. This reduces the starting capital to a bare minimum. The Dropshipping model ensures that you make a sale first before buying it from the supplier and even then, the burden of packaging and shipping lies with the third party. The cost of running the business is also low as there is no physical store to run. Overhead expenses like rent, employees' salaries, office supplies, and licenses are not something a drop shipper has to worry about. They only need a computer, reliable internet connection and a website to do their business which is monthly services and can be accessed at a low cost

2. It is an easy business to start

Compared to many businesses today, starting a Drop shipping business can be easy. Everything you need to know about running an online business can be accessed online. You can also keep improving your marketing skill after starting the business as there is nothing for you to lose. Compared to business people with an inventory, you don't need to worry about stock taking, office management. As you will not be handling any inventory, the stress of replacing finished products, packing and shipping orders to clients or getting a warehouse is not yours. Making sure orders get to the clients and dealing with returns is also someone else's business.

3. You are not bound to any location

You can start a Drop shipping business anywhere in the world as long as you have a laptop and a strong internet connection. With the availability of large e-commerce stores that can help you connect with manufacturers directly, you can do business with anyone in the world today. Payments can also be made online without the merchant, customer and the manufacturer ever meeting face to face. All you need is trust and reliability coupled with connectivity to the internet.

4. You can sell a wide range of items

A standard retailer worries about space and cost of purchasing inventory when deciding what they want to sell. This is not the case with drop shippers. All they need to do is check if the client has the product in stock and then they put it up on the website for sale. A drop shipper can have different categories and selections for different customers as long as the third party can supply it to the customer.

5. It takes a short time for the new business to scale upward

The problem standard retail model is that with more customers, the processing of orders increases and thus the need to hire more stuff. This burden is absent in this case as, despite the increase in orders, it's the supplier that deals with packaging and shipping. This doesn't affect the merchant in any way except maybe making payments more frequently which hardly seems like a con. The other work that may increase maybe in customer care but that can be solved with one employee or two.

Disadvantages of Dropshipping

1. Some niches have low-profit margins

Depending on the niche that you choose to go into, there is the possibility of making a little profit per item. In the beginning, the merchant may under-price to get traffic to the website. He or she will have to sell a lot of products so that they can make more money in the long run which can take a while to happen. There is also a lot of competition online, and the customers will end up picking the website that offers the lowest price.

2. You have to choose the right supplier

Unless you have the utmost trust that your supplier will deliver the products to the customers at the right time and in the right condition, your business is bound to fail. Standard retailers don't face this problem as they can assure quality control in their inventory and shipping process. You will, therefore, need to experiment until you get the right partner. Customer complaints will most definitely be directed towards you despite the mishap not being our fault. Ensure you communicate with your suppliers constantly to improve the shipping process and reduce complaints.

3. The challenges of dealing with multiple suppliers

As a drop shipper, it isn't uncommon to deal with many suppliers at the same time. Some may be dependable, but some may not, and the customer may buy items that come from different suppliers. First, there may be significant differences in shipping costs that may not make sense to the customer. Computing different shipping charges from different suppliers may be hard because the cost may be too much for a customer to handle. You may, therefore, have to standardize the charges which may come from your pocket.

Despite being an easy way to make passive income, Drop shipping requires a lot of dedication and hard work. It is not a get rich quick scheme. These challenges can be overcome if the merchant uses different strategies from everyone else.

Chapter 2
Affiliate Marketing

Residual income is passive income that comes in every month whether you show up or not. It's when you no longer get paid on your personal efforts alone, but you get paid on the efforts of hundreds or even thousands of others and your money! It's one of the keys to financial freedom and time freedom.

-Steve Fisher

Affiliate marketing is the perfect way to make extra money. With affiliate marketing, you earn money by putting your audience onto a company's product, and if they end up buying, you earn a commission. You are like a middle man between a consumer and a company. You will need to understand the four players in the entire affiliate marketing process.

- The product creator or the seller is the person that owns a certain brand and could benefit from people buying their product.

- An affiliate network is a program that links product creators to interests affiliate marketers. Even though the product creator can get affiliate marketers on their own, it is safer for the affiliate marketer to use an affiliate link. They can track their earnings and ensure they are paid on time through a legitimate affiliate network.

- An affiliate marketer is a person that takes advantage of an offer to market products from a product creator to get people to but their product in exchange for a percentage of the sale. They are in charge of aggressive marketing as they earn from what they sell. A super affiliate is someone who is driving up the sales of the product they promote.

- The end consumer who buys the product promoted by the affiliate marketer.

In affiliate marketing, you can make money as both a product creator or as an affiliate marketer.

4 Steps to Become a Product Creator

A product creator can be known by many names. They include seller, merchant, a brand, vendor or retailer. As a seller, you make a product and have an affiliate marker sell it for you.

Step 1: Look for a great product idea

As a seller, don't jump into creating a product without thinking the idea through. Think of a product that many people need in their life and solves a certain problem they have. Take time to perfect the idea to come up with a product people are willing to buy. Look into products in popular niches that people are searching for online. Instead of coming up with an idea from thin air, consider looking at what already exists in the market and improve on it. Don't be rigid when it comes to ideas; change your mind depending on what you learn about a certain niche. It is always better to look for inspiration from things that you are already interested in or knowledgeable about. This saves you time as you know the important basics that you will need to build upon.

Step 2: Research to see if people like the idea and if there is a need it fills

After getting the idea that you want to pursue, carry out market research to see if people would buy. The market is the true test of a successful product, and people would buy what they want as opposed to what you are selling to them. You can use available research tools like Buzzsumo to know what people are currently into. Once you are sure, you can test the market by asking people if they would buy the product. If so, let them preorder so that you can see if they would spend money on your product.

Step 3: Make the product

There are many resources online that tell you exactly how to create great digital products. Whether its online courses and webinars, instructional eBooks or podcasts; follow instructions from people who are knowledgeable in each field make a useful product that solves a problem. Remember to deliver the finished product to the buyers that pre-ordered and get some feedback on it. Create a website that allows people to learn more about your product and buy it.

Step 4: Join an affiliate network or look for affiliate marketers to market your product

It's finally time to bring in affiliates on board. You can join an affiliate network and connect to affiliates. One thing you have to keep in mind is that the most useful affiliates are the ones already in your niche. They already have an audience that wants to buy products like yours, and this can translate into sales for your product. So how can you get affiliate marketers in your niche? Search online for pop up sites that are in the same niche as you and pitch to them a collaboration.

A good thing to remember is that if your product goes deep in a certain niche, the easier it will be to get fellow merchants to support you. A proposal on a prospective partnership should detail how both of you will benefit in the long run. For you get people who are willing to market your product, you have to give them a good deal on the commission. If you offer commissions between 45-60%, then more people will be willing to come on board. The reason big companies offer low commissions is that they have many affiliate marketers and their product is easy to market as people already know the product. Since your product is new, you will not get the same result if you are stingy with pay-outs. They are even more likely to work harder to bring in customers as they are motivated. Look for YouTube channels in the same niche and tell them about your product and make them an offer.

If you have a website already, start writing blog posts telling people about your product and mention that you would also like affiliate marketers to come on board. Growing an email list and sharing on your social media platforms can also attract some affiliate marketers.

4 Ways to Make Money as an Affiliate Marketer

1. Join an Affiliate network

Joining an affiliate program enables you to see products that are on sale and need affiliate marketing. When you choose an affiliate program, for example, Amazon Associates, you can get a sharable affiliate link that you can share with your audience that they can click to buy. That is the link that identifies you and is the one you will use in all your marketing strategies.

2. Review products online

People lie to see what they are buying and what better way to do that than watching someone testing it for them. By showing people how good the product is, you will capture their attention such that when you give them a call to action to buy the product, they will do just that. Ensure you give honest reviews and sell only products you are sure about. That is the only way you will become an authority in your niche. I think by now you know you have to pick a niche and stick to it. You can write your review on a website or make a video review and post on YouTube. A clever way to make more money is to do multiple reviews in one and put all the affiliate links in the post for people to choose what they like best. On your website, you can have links to products you have tried, tested and loved. They can be products, resources or other items you feel confident about.

3. Comparing products

This is a good way to get people to buy using your link as there are many similar products that people find it hard to choose from. If a person stumbles upon your post, they will most likely buy because they were searching for the best of the two or three products. The comparison has to offer in-depth insight into both products and consider giving them an honest recommendation.

4. E-mail marketing

This is a popular marketing strategy that has earned some affiliate marketers 6 figure commissions. For any affiliate marketer, a community of people that respect and trust your opinion is vital as they are likely to be your customers when you suggest a product. The bigger your email list the more leverage you have when you have a product to promote. But how can you build an email list that you can convert into a loyal customer base? First, you will need software that creates for you a landing page and an automated response email marketing tool.

Remember that people will subscribe to your email list if you offer them something that they need. It shouldn't always be about selling something to them but rather appreciate them by giving them lead magnets. A lead magnet is a tool used by affiliate marketers to attract people to sign up for an email list. They include free courses, planners and budgeting tools, eBooks pretty much anything you can think of that people would want so that they keep looking out for more of it. A good lead magnet is free, simple to understand, straight to the point, related to the website niche and most importantly it should provide value to the customer. When you create a lead magnet, get its special URL and upload it to an accessible site. A tip here is to cleverly add your affiliate links in your lead magnet to maximize profits.

Remember we talked about landing pages earlier, but it has other names too. It is also called a capture, squeeze or lead page. Its main aim is to attract the visitor and make him, or she sign up with their email. Whatever the software or design you use, you then connect the landing page with your email collecting tool.

Automation is the heart and soul of passive income and in affiliate marketing in particular. You don't need to be constantly typing and updating content for your email list when you can schedule content and still be effective in other areas. In email marketing, get an autoresponder that follows up with a series of emails that add value to your subscribers and subtly reminds them of what you are selling. Don't spam peoples mail as they will surely unsubscribe. Keep them interested with more free stuff, and use language then makes them feel like your friend and not a customer.

Advantages of Affiliate Marketing

1. Low overhead and cheap to start

Whether you decide to become a product creator or an affiliate marketer, you only need a computer, a website or YouTube channel and internet connection. The only payment you will make as for hosting the website.

2. Products are digital

Digital products are cheap to create because they don't occupy space in a warehouse, and they don't require shipping to reach the consumer. In case someone is an affiliate marketer, they do not need to create any product at all, therefore, saving themselves some time.

3. It's flexible

Compared to other businesses and jobs, there is no designated time or place that one should be at to succeed. As long as you have a steady internet connection and are dedicated, you shall succeed. There is also no limit to the number of affiliate products you can market at the same time. Automation means that you can earn even when you are offline.

4. Earning potential

As I stated before, people are making 6-7 figure incomes by promoting products online. Depending on your strategies towards earning a passive income, nothing is stopping you from making a living out of affiliate marketing.

5. It can be done parallel to other online businesses.

Many people are doing online business, and affiliate marketing can be integrated into another income stream. Since all you require is an affiliate link that can be placed anywhere on a website, it doesn't have to interfere with anything. Email marketing is automated; therefore one can earn without checking in.

Disadvantages of Affiliate Marketing

1. It takes some time before someone gets to earn money. For those who think that affiliate marketing is getting rich quick scheme, they shall be disappointed as some people have stayed for a year before making any money. It requires patience and perseverance.

2. As with any money-making venture, some people hijack your

affiliate, and you don't get your commission when they use your link. To be safe, you can try using URL masking to protect your affiliate links from cybercriminals.

3. Choosing a bad affiliate company can tarnish your reputation and will lead to mistrust among your loyal followers. Ensure you work with brands that have the same value as you.

4. You cannot analyze the numbers apart from the traffic that is going to the product site, sales, and returns. You won't know anything else about the customer. Therefore, marketing will always be by chance. You are not a part of the business module unless you are the product creator.

5. Unless you are in a reputable affiliate network, you may not be paid for your work, and there is no way to track down the company.

6. It is a competitive space to be in especially if a company is offering a high commission. The challenge is how you can market the product while standing out from the rest.

Mistakes to Avoid as A New Affiliate Marketer

Don't be that person that is only looking to make a quick buck from people. People can always tell if all you are doing is pushing a product instead of being yourself. Don't think of yourself as a seller of the product but as an influence of people towards a product. All you have to do is offer a suggestion with all the relevant facts and let the people decide. If you can, test out the products first before recommending them to your loyal subscribers to avoid unforeseen problems. Don't embellish or oversell something if you are not sure how it works. It is a sure way to lose credibility.

Pick one affiliate program and perfect that instead of joining multiple programs. As a beginner, you are still wet behind the ears, and you need to learn and make mistakes before you can fill your plate with more work. Learn from other people doing the same thing on the internet and be good at one thing first. You will find out that you can make more money that way than dipping your toe in everything.

If you are promoting multiple products, track each one of them so that you can drop whatever is not earning you anything. There is no need to keep pushing something that is not converting well in sales. With a good affiliate network like Amazon, they offer unique tracking IDs that can help you manage all your links.

Avoid changing niches at all costs. When you have good subscribership, they expect something from you, and that is why they are following you. Even if you suspect something is better than what you are currently doing, make a different site for it instead of confusing your followers. See one thing through before moving on to something else.

Chapter 3
Passive Income Investments

Compound interest is the eighth wonder of the world. He who understands it earns it ... he who doesn't ... pays it. Compound interest is the most powerful force in the universe. Compound interest is the greatest mathematical discovery of all time.

- Albert Einstein

What Are Passive Income Investments?

Passive income investing is where you put up your money in capital investments such as mutual funds, treasury bonds, and bills, fixed accounts and even stocks. You earn an income from either earning a percentage of the company you are investing in or you earn dividends or interest from the money you choose to invest. Here, you are just financing the investing and not directly managing it, making it passive. You will be earning residual income that is calculated by compounding what you choose to invest. As a beginner, you will only put in your money once into a passive income investment and from there on out, you will have regular deposits from your investments.

People who are working tend to ignore the fact that they won't be working forever. They need to start planning for retirement by looking into their income, their daily expenses and how much money they can save to maintain the same lifestyle when they retire. Young people are notorious for living large and forgetting that this is the best time to start saving as they have no real obligations. Investing doesn't have an age limit. Some parents open up education funds for their children as soon as they born and save. This reduces the burden when the time comes to pay from school. Some teach the importance of saving by opening for them their own savings accounts. What they need to do is teach them that money can also grow on its own if placed in the right places. These children then grow while learning to invest so that they make more money.

11 Examples of Passive Income Investments

1. Crowdfunded Real Estate

For many years, we have believed that becoming a real estate mogul requires a lot of capital to get into. An easier way to get into real estate is by investing in crowdfunded ventures. There are multiple companies like Fundraiser that allow you to deposit as low as $500 and get a stake in at least 48 real estate projects. There are some companies like Rich Uncles that you can register for free that offer even more affordable options. Rich Uncles, for example, has an offer called Student Housing REIT (Real Estate Investment Trust) that one can invest as little as $5. Many companies are trying to bring real estate investments more mainstream and are targeting low-income earners.

2. Certificate of Deposit (CDs) Ladders

CDs are a great way for beginners to start because there are no minimums in what one can start with compared to many other capital investments. The fact that they are also available in local banks is perfect as you can open a CD account easily. It is low risk because an FDIC insures individual CDs for up to $250,000 and joint accounts for up to $500,000. It's relatively easy to withdraw your money from a CD and is a great way to earn an income with minimum effort. The longer the CD like five years or more, the higher the interest the bank offers on it. You can buy CDs in online banks such as CIT bank.

3. Dividend Income

When you invest in a company by buying the shares or stocks in that company, then you earn a dividend based on the number of shares you have. If you want to learn a lot about investment, you might want to follow the billionaire investor Warren Buffet as he has a lot of wisdom to share in the subject. Dividends can be paid quarterly or annually depending on the company in question. Before investing in a company, look at their history and expert predictions on their future so that you don't end up investing in a company that won't be around for a long time. To make more money, consider investing for the long haul. To invest in stocks, open an investment account with a licensed stockbroker so that your investment is safe. You will have to pay a small fee to buy stocks, but that is all. Keep looking into good companies to invest in as you build your portfolio.

4. Bonds (Fixed Income)

Bonds are great as their interest rates were going up for the past few years. Even if the interest rates remain steady or go up, bonds are a good way to earn passive income, especially if you hold them until they mature. They are good for long term investors who will not withdraw the money before the maturity period is up. There are different bonds to choose from such as an individual corporate bond, the 7-10-year IEF, municipal bonds or the Pimco Total Return Fund which is a fixed income fund.

5. Peer to Peer Lending (P2P)

You can become a shylock of some sort, i.e., lending to people who need credit but cannot get it from traditional loan institutions. Some companies that allow you to invest in their peer to peer lending business with low costing bonds (as low as $10) and paying out returns ranging from 3-8%. They have no restriction on when you can have your money back. You can just walk in and withdraw any amount you want. It is a risky business as some borrowers will not pay back the money they borrow. You will also need to invest a lot more money to get high-interest rates.

6. Private Equity Investments

Some people had struck big because they believed in the vision of start-ups early on before they blew up. Look at the people that bought into Facebook, Uber, Amazon, Alibaba, Google and many others before they became the giants they are today. It is tough today to know which company would blow up. Therefore, you can choose to go the way other private investment firms are going. This is however not for everyone as it is limited to approved investors. They mostly invest in hedge funds, real estate, and other private companies. It is good for long term investors, and you will find more passive income. The risk depends on the company you are investing in, i.e., if it is in a competitive field like finance. Real estate and fixed income funds can give up to 8-15% interest on investments.

7. High-Yield Online Accounts

If you are looking into a low-risk investment, open an FDIC insured high yield online account with banks like CIT Bank that offer up to 2.45% interest rates. You will not earn a lot of money at once, but in the long term, you will have earned much more than if you put your money in a normal savings account. Online banks offer good interest rates as they do not have a lot of overhead to keep operating. They can pay 19 times the interest most traditional banks to pay.

8. Money Market Funds

A money market fund is perfect for beginners who have no idea what investing is all about. All you have to do is look for a reputable money market fund that offers good returns, and they will do all the thinking for you. They are located in banks and other investment agencies. There are some types of mutual funds called index funds that mirror the market index they are tied to. These funds track a certain index thus doesn't need a lot of management because the underlying index rarely changes. The fees for this fund is low, and the lower turnover means that the tax will less too. Lower taxes mean higher returns for the investor.

9.   Owning a Real Estate Property

It would be unwise to assume that all beginners have no money to make big investments such as real estate. Owning a real estate property and earning a rental income has been done for a long time and it works. If you have a spare room, you can rent it out to a trustworthy tenant. You can also own a rental property and earn a steady income while it keeps increasing in value. Remember that your rental income would be subject to taxes, mortgages, insurance, and operational costs. The rental income in cities can be low because the expenses are high despite the rental income being high as well. This means that the risk of owning rental property in an expensive city is higher than owning one in a cheaper area. The same applies in areas with insecurity even with property insurance. You can also buy houses fix them up for sale at a higher cost. This is a great way to earn more money even though you may need to be involved even if you hire someone to help you out. The return is amazing, and the risk is moderate depending on the location of the property.

10. Annuities

They are offered by insurance companies where you have to pay a certain amount every month, and in return, they pay you monthly dividends. It is always better to talk to a professional finance officer before investing in annuities because not all of them are as good as they sound. Look at the terms before buying because some charge a lot and may not be a good investment. It is okay if you are looking for a zero-risk investment and want to be earning an income for a long time.

11. Pay Off Your Debts

You can be earning a steady passive income, but if all of it is going towards repaying debts and mortgages then, you are not benefitting at all. For mortgages, look for companies that are offering better rates than your current financiers. There are services online that help you compare rates for different mortgage lenders such as LendingTree. If you are repaying a credit card debt or loan at an interest rate of 12%, the good thing about repaying it is that you get a 12% straight return. You may not necessarily have a lot of money at hand. Therefore, it is better to look at two possible approaches. One is the one we have talked about earlier on refinancing the debt to one that offers a lower interest rate. The second way is to consolidate two debts and pay the two together at a lower interest rate. The third way is to register for a balance transfer card that allows you to pay off the debt within a specified period at no extra cost.

Advantages

1. You can choose what works for you. Depending on your income bracket, there are many investment options out there for you.

2. Building your investment portfolio can be an asset in the long run as you can leverage it when you need to. You may even retire if your passive investments make enough money for you to live comfortably on.

3. It is perfect for people who don't understand anything about the

markets. Most of the investment is often made by trained professionals making it perfect for earning without managing anything. It is safe to say that even though someone else handles your investments, you should keep track to see if you are gaining or losing.

4. Long term investors benefit more from investments because they earn more dividends. Also, some funds also give better interest rates for investors.

Disadvantages

1. It is not exactly the quickest way to make money. It requires patience and a sound strategy to earn a good income even in the long term.

2. Even though some investments promise high yield, if you look at the return you get in the long haul, you will realize that it was not worth your time in the first place. This means that before investing, a professional would help you better understand the projections before you commit your money in a venture that won't give you high returns eventually.

3. For a beginner with little money and no expertise, high returns may be elusive. Those who earn better incomes are those who are willing to risk a lot and work to get better deals. Research and participation may be the only way to earn a better income.

4. Investing can be quite a hard topic for people who are not into finance and economics. There are hard terms to understand, and the mathematics can be even more confusing but what separates someone who makes a wise investment from one who goes with the wind is some basic form of investing knowledge.

5. Some people ignore retirement accounts as a form of investing and yet they are low risk and are taxed a lot less than other investment accounts. Good retirement funds include 401(k)s and Roth IRAs.

6. Most people just put away money in investment accounts and forget to use some of it. It is okay to use some of the money you earn on yourself. Don't wait until you are too old to enjoy the money that you have worked so hard because other people will.

Check Out Our Other AMAZING Titles:

1. Resolving Anxiety and Panic Attacks

A Guide to Overcoming Severe Anxiety, Controlling Panic Attacks and Reclaiming Your Life Again

Worldwide, one in six people is affected by a mental health disorder. So you are not alone in this (Ritchie & Roser, 2019). There is a difference between clinical anxiety and everyday anxiety. Everyday anxiety is normal and in often cases, it is necessary, while chronic anxiety will leave you functionally impaired. This book will not only inform you about anxiety and panic attacks but also introduce you to various methods and techniques that aid in getting rid of anxiety. It is a perfect package if you want to make long-lasting, meaningful changes in your life in a way that gets rid of anxiety. Knowledge is power, so gaining information about anxiety and panic attacks already puts you in the lead against them.

In the first chapter, we'll start with the basic knowledge of panic attacks and anxiety. The symptoms of both are pretty much the same, but there are some major differences as well. Knowing their difference and similarities can help you clearly understand your condition. Some basic ways of coping with them are also explained alongside their symptoms.

After gaining knowledge about anxiety and panic attacks in the first section, you will seek answers and ways to overcome them. The second chapter goes more in detail about the physical effects of anxiety. There are some types of anxiety which are also talked briefly about in the chapter. There are also therapies and treatments that are used to overcome and control anxiety. Their details are discussed in the chapter from where you can figure out what sort of treatment will suit you better. Some other ways of coping with anxiety are also discussed and they will surely prove beneficial to the reader.

The third chapter will make you aware of how interrelated physical and mental healths are. There are also details on how to improve one's physical health to influence a person's anxiety positively. You will also learn how important practicing well-being is. If you are to ignore physical health, it will cause problems for your mental health as well.

The fourth chapter will delve deep into mindfulness and its vast benefits. Mindfulness is a very powerful tool we have but don't know how to use. It can be practiced through meditation techniques, etc. It makes us see things more clearly than ever before. Practicing Mindfulness will arm you against any anxiety and panic attacks. In this chapter, it is explained in detail what it means and what are its advantages.

In the fifth chapter, we will learn about meditation and how can it help manage anxiety. We first start off by knowing what it is. You also have got to know its benefits and various techniques from which one can pick according to their choice. We will also learn the accurate posture you should have during meditation. We will learn how mediation reinforces our brain to stave off anxiety and panic attacks. It is a long road but a successful one for sure. Besides helping us out with anxiety and panic disorder, meditation has numerous other benefits for our body and mind.

The sixth chapter will explore the meaning behind self-love and its importance in fighting anxiety. Our battle with anxiety has to start from a positive ground. We first have to be fully comfortable and respectful towards ourselves. You will also find out how lack of self-love can actually breed anxiety.

Opening about anxiety is not an easy task but could be very helpful against anxiety. How to go about the whole process is talked about in detail in the seventh chapter. You will also learn how to evaluate your therapist and choose the right one. In this chapter, there are also guidelines for people who have just recently become aware of their anxiety and now they want to seek help. It will give them knowledge about things to consider when talking to someone about mental health, what you should accept and be prepared for. There is also information about talk therapy there.

In the eighth chapter, we address the misunderstanding about anxiety. Despite affecting so many people, it remains a different experience for all of them. There are also common mistakes pointed out in that chapter which we'll go into detail the mistakes that make our anxiety worse.

The ninth chapter is about where we talk about putting our foot down and start to incorporate practices into our life which will help you get rid of anxiety and panic attacks. We will learn how to manage our responses. It is basically a comprehensive listing of all the things you should be avoiding or adapting to lead a healthy lifestyle free of anxiety.

Want to read more? Purchase our book on **Anxiety and Panic Attacks** *today!*

2. Cognitive Behavioral Therapy

How CBT Can Be Used to Rewire Your Brain, Stop Anxiety, and Overcome Depression

Cognitive stems from cognition, which encapsulates the idea of how we learn and the knowledge that we carry. The things you learn are part of your cognition, and what you do with that information is included in that category as well. Cognition includes a wide list of information that you might not fully realize.

Behavior is what we do. It is how we act. The things that you choose to say to other people are all about your behavior. How you react to what others have to say will exhibit your behavior as well. Your behavior is all about your mind interacting with your body and how that interacts with the people and other things that surround you.

Therapy is any form of help, usually from a trained professional, to help improve on whatever the therapy is specified for. You might get physical therapy to help regain strength in your knee after having a serious surgery. You can also get therapy to help overcome an alcohol or drug addiction.

Throughout this book, we're going to give you the basis you need to start understanding cognitive behavioral therapy. The three together—cognitive, behavioral, therapy—all make up CBT, which is a method that is going to directly help you overcome the mental illness that you are hoping to treat.

Therapy can be expensive, and even if you do have the means to go through with this process, you might struggle to find the right therapist. Sometimes, you might live in an area where there is only one therapist within a close distance, but you don't have a vibe with them that you find to be helpful. You might also find that you are desperate for help and that you want a therapist, but insurance coverage isn't always good for this.

By reading this book, you'll be able to find the tools you need to help with overcoming your most challenging thoughts. We are going to take you through the steps to identify the root issues and come up with specific methods to get you through.

*Want to read more? Purchase our book on **Cognitive Behavioral Therapy** today!*

3. Effective Guide On How to Sleep Well Everyday

The Easy Method For Better Sleep, Insomnia And Chronic Sleep Problems

"A well spent day brings happy sleep."

— Leonardo da Vinci

Are you experiencing the worst restless feeling? Has your doctor diagnosed you with insomnia, restlessness, sleeplessness? When the whole world around you seems to be in peaceful deep slumber, you are the one who is restless. No matter what term is used to describe it, the fact is that it is you who is actually going through insomnia, and nothing could feel worse than that.

So you drag yourself from bed in the morning feeling as earth, with its entire lock stock and barrel, has decided to perch on your head for the day. Yet you go through the motions of the day, though you barely manage to make it through the hours. By the early night, you fall on to bed hoping this night will be different because you're dead tired and nothing will keep you from sleeping like a log. It's 2.00 a.m. now, dawn is breaking through and there you are, still wide awake and ready to scream to the world because no matter how tired you are or how hard you have tried, you simply can't get to sleep.

While there are proven facts and evidence of the devastating effects of sleeping less, the investigations are still on to establish the exact nature of effects resulting from too much sleep. Some researchers argue that people

210

who sleep much longer than necessarily have a higher death rate. Physical and mental conditions such as depression or socioeconomic status can also lead to excessive sleep. There are other researchers who argue that the human body will naturally restrain it from sleeping more hours than really necessary. However, with research still underway for concrete evidence of the effects of over sleeping the best path you can choose is to adopt a sleeping pattern somewhere in the middle. According to the National Sleep Foundation, this middle range falls between seven and eight hours of sleep during the night. Despite these statistics, the best way to ensure you receive sufficient sleeping time is to let your own body act as your guide. You can always sleep a little extra if you feel exhausted or sleep a little less than usual if you feel you are oversleeping.

Dangers of Sleep deprivation.

Though sleep is something the average human being takes for granted, it is also one of the greatest mysteries in life. Just like we still don't have all the answers to the quantum field or gravity, researchers are still exploring the reasons behind the 'whats' and 'whys' of sleep. However, one fact unchallenged about sleep is that a proper sleep is paramount for maintaining good health. The general guideline regarding the optimal amount of sleep for an adult range from six to eight hours! If you carry on with too little or too much of this general guideline you are exposing yourself to the risk of adverse health effects.

Though sleep is something that comes naturally to many people, the problems of sleep deprivation have today become a pressing problem with more and more people succumbing to chronic sleeping disorders. Unfortunately, a great number of these people do not even realize that lack of sleep or sleep deprivation is at the root of their manifold problems in life. Scientific research also points out that lack of sleep on a continuous scale can lead to severe repercussions on your health.

If you have been experiencing impaired sleep patterns for a longer period, you also face the risk of:

- Severely impairing your immunity strength

- Promoting the risk of tumor growth, as it has been scientifically established that a tumor can grow at least two to three times faster among animals subjected to severe sleeping dysfunctions within a laboratory setting.

- Creating a pre-diabetic condition in the body. Insomnia creates hunger, making you want to eat even when you have already had a meal. This situation can lead to problems of obesity in turn.

- Critically impairing memory. How many times during the day have you found it difficult to remember even the most mundane and repetitive events when you have had no more than 4 – 5 hours of sleep? Even a single night of impaired sleep plays havoc with our memory faculties, just think what it can do to your brain if you consistently lose sleep.

- Ruining your performance level both physically and mentally as your problem-solving abilities will not be working in peak order.

- Stomach ulcers

- Constipation, hemorrhoids

- Heart diseases

- Depression, lethargy and other mood disorders

- Daytime drowsiness

- Irritability

- Low energy

- Low mental clarity

- Reaction time slows down

- Lower productivity

- More accidents and mistakes

- Lower levels of growth hormone and testosterone

The growth hormone in the body which is vital for maintaining our looks, energy, and skin texture is produced by the pituitary gland. The specialty of this hormone production procedure is that it is only produced during the times of deep slumber or during intense workout sessions. In the absence of normal production of the growth hormone, our bodies will start on a premature aging process. According to research, people suffering from chronic insomnia are three times more susceptible to contract fatal diseases. When you lose sleep overnight, you cannot make up for it by sleeping more the next day. A night's lost sleep will be lost forever. More alarmingly if you continue to lose sleep regularly, they will create a cumulative negative effect that will disrupt your general health. All in all, sleeping deficiencies can effectively make your life miserable, as you already know.

How Much Sleep Do I Really Need?

This is a question that remains a mystery just like the questions of why and what makes us want to sleep. In response to a question of how many hours of sleep do we really need, an expert has answered that it is actually lot less than what we have been taught. On the other hand, though a good night's sleep is vital for good health, overdoing the sleeping can be equally bad for us. But if you sleep less and continue this for too long, the result will be confusion between body and brain signals, resulting in muddled thoughts, lethargic feelings, and overall lassitude. So, the question remains, how many hours of sleep do we really need? Is it essential to sleep the prescribed number of eight hours a day or is catching up a good sleep on a five to six-hour basis enough?

The eight hours of sleep theory is increasingly becoming unpractical in this fast-paced lifestyle. Actually, the recommendation of eight hours of sleep arises based on the idea that our ancestors had their beauty sleep between 8-9 hours in the past. In today's context, this concept is regarded more or less as a myth. In a study conducted by the Sleep Research Center, youngsters within the age group of 8 to 17 generally sleep for about nine hours during the night. However, in the case of adults, this theory is not applicable as a majority of them are sleepless and many of them thrive after a solid sleep varying between 5-7 hours.

A research conducted by the National Institute of Health has established that people who sleep soundly for nine hours a day or more are actually two times more vulnerable than those who sleep less in developing Parkinson's disease. A study report released by the Diabetes Care states that people claiming to sleep less than five hours or more than nine hours daily are the ones with the highest risk of attracting diabetes. In contrast, a large number of contemporary studies prove that people with sleeping patterns that do not exceed or fall beyond seven hours daily possess the highest survival rate. The persons who experience sleeping disorders and sleep less than 4.5 hours have the worst survival rate.

When ascertaining the correct number of hours you should sleep, the fact is that there is no magic number of hours. It will depend on a person to person basis as well as factors like age, activity, and performance level. For example, smaller children and teenagers require more sleep compared to adults. Your personal requirements will not be the same as your friend or colleague who is of the same age and gender as you. Because your sleep needs are unique and individual. According to the National Sleep Foundation, the difference of sleep requirements between two people of the same age, gender, and activity level is due to their basal sleep needs and sleep debt.

Your basal sleep need is the number of hours of sleep you typically need to engage in optimal performance levels. The sleep debt comprises of the accumulated number of hours of sleep you have lost as a result of poor sleeping habits, a recent sickness, social demands, environmental factors, etc. A healthy adult generally possesses a basal sleep need between seven and eight hours each night. If you have experienced sleeping difficulties and as a result accumulated a sleep debt you will find that your performance level is not up to its usual standard, even if you wake up after seven or eight hours of restful sleep. The symptoms will be most apparent during the times the circadian rhythm naturally alters like during mid-afternoon or overnight. One of the ways of easing out of an accumulated sleep debt situation is to get a few extra hours of sleep for a couple of nights until you regain your natural sleeping rhythm and vitality during the day.

Understand what Kind of a Sleeper Are You?

Sleep, dear reader, is the precious restorative that rights so many physical and mental wrongs. The elixir that transforms life and puts a spring in your step, a smile on your face, and the feeling that you can take care of everything that comes your way is sleep. Undervalued, ignored, and forgotten until you wake up to the realization that it's one of the essential foundations of daily wellbeing.

So what kind of a sleeper are you? There are many studies and descriptions of how we sleep but the common consensus settles for the following five simple categories:

1. Lively, healthy early risers!

These happy individuals usually get the sleep they need and rarely feel exhausted or fatigued. They are typically younger than the other groups, usually married or with a long-term partner, working full-time and definitely a morning person with no serious medical conditions.

2. Relaxed and retired seniors.

This is the oldest group in the survey with half of the sample being 65 or older. They sleep the most with an average of 7.3 hours per night compared to 6.8 across all groups. Sleep disorders are rare even though there is a significant proportion with at least one medical disorder.

3. Dozing drones.

These busy people are usually married/partnered and employed but they often work much longer than forty hours a week. Frequently working up to the hour when they go to bed, they get up early so they're always short of sleep and struggle to keep up with the daily pressures of life. Statistically, they'll feel tired or fatigued at least three days a week.

4. Galley slaves.

This group works the longest hours and often suffers from weight problems as well as an unhealthy reliance on caffeine to get through the day. Shift workers often fall into this group and there is also a marked tendency to be a night owl or evening person. They get the least amount of sleep and are more likely to take naps yet, surprisingly, this group often believes that, despite the state of their health, they are getting enough sleep.

5. Insomniacs.

Here is the largest proportion of night people and many of them quite rightly believe they have a sleep problem. About half of this group feels they get less sleep than they need and the same proportion admits to feeling tired, fatigued and lacking energy most of the time.

So, which of the five groups do you think you fit into?

If you're a happy member of Group One, your sleep should by definition be absolutely fine. Don't worry. We've got some really good ideas to share with you to keep you right on track and we'll even add some special extra features to your nightly rest routine to maximize the experience. If you're not in this group, our aim is to help you become a full-time member of the healthy, happy sleepers' association! Membership is for life.

Group Three represents too many tired, irritable, and generally inefficient individuals whose quality of life is impaired because they're too tired too often. Their work suffers because they rarely have sufficient rest to successfully assimilate the day's events. Their home life is degraded because work intrudes too often and they're just too tired to enjoy the pleasures and comfort of a life away from work. Feeling tired becomes their default position and they know they need to do something to give their minds and bodies the rest they deserve. Individuals in this group frequently suffer from long- term mental, physical and emotional stress.

The fourth group is rightly described as the night owls. They work the longest hours and, as we noted above, they typically work shifts. The health problems associated with this group include a marked tendency towards obesity as well as a range of inflammatory diseases. Despite the fact that these people rarely look or feel well, they seem to ignore the evidence and usually claim to get enough sleep, relying on sugary energy drinks and caffeine to keep them awake during waking hours. They take naps because their bodies can't function without additional sleep during the day. An objective analysis of their health would typically reveal a range of health and wellbeing issues.

Insomniacs are the dominant members of Group Five, people who don't get enough sleep, can't get to sleep, and who know they have a problem. Unfortunately, many insomniacs end up taking prescription medication to deal with their symptoms and we have to question the benefits of this solution in light of the many unpleasant side effects associated with long-term sleeping pill dependency. For insomniacs, life is a constant struggle because of the accumulative effects of long-term sleep deprivation.

Health issues abound, depression becomes a major risk, their ability to function normally is often impaired, and they lose sight of their potential to deal successfully with life's daily challenges. They sometimes refer to their condition as living in a nightmare world where they are constantly exhausted and simply cannot function. It's completely understandable that a doctor would prescribe sleeping drugs because the dangers of sleep deprivation can be acute.

Before we begin to examine the practicalities of sleep, we need to know how much sleep is appropriate for each of us as individuals. It's not surprising that different age groups have different sleep requirements.

For example, very young children and infants can sleep in total for around 14 - 15 hours a day. And if you've got teenagers, you might have guessed that adolescents usually need more sleep than adults. Teens can easily sleep between 8.5 to 9.5 hours a night.

It's widely understood that during the first trimester, pregnant women often find they need a lot more sleep than usual. The fact is that if you feel tired during the day, find yourself yawning or taking a nap, you're short on sleep. And this is the time for you to do something practical, realistic, and effective to take care of the problem.

There are many myths surrounding the condition known as OAS or Obstructive Sleep Apnea. It's estimated that around 18 million Americans suffer from the condition but the numbers could be much higher because many people don't report the condition to their doctors. This condition is far more than just loud snoring, although snoring can be a sign of sleep apnea.

People with this condition skip breathing 400 times during the night. The delay in breathing can last from ten to thirty seconds and is then followed by a loud snore as breathing suddenly resumes. The normal sleep cycle is interrupted and this can leave sufferers feeling tired and exhausted during the day. It is a serious condition, especially since it can lead to accidents at work, problems when driving, as well as increasing the risk of heart attacks and strokes. It can affect people of all ages, including children, but tends to affect people more after the age of forty.

Weight also plays a part and there is evidence that shedding excess pounds can improve the condition. Despite all the advice and overwhelming evidence, there are still surprising numbers of sleep apnea sufferers who continue to smoke. Smoking is a perfect way to increase the severity and risks of this debilitating condition.

If you've already trimmed your weight, quit smoking and tried sleeping on your side but still suffer from the condition, you need to see your doctor. There are many treatments available including a special mask that delivers constant air flow to keep the breathing passage open. Lifestyle choices can clearly make a positive difference, too.

Your body, your brain, your mind and your emotional functioning all rely on sufficient sleep to operate efficiently. If you don't get enough sleep, everything suffers. Research suggests that it's much harder than you might imagine to adapt having less sleep than your body needs. The sleep deficit has to be repaid at some point or we'll experience increasingly severe problems.

Simple techniques of preparing for bed

1. Try to get to bed early. The recharging of the body's adrenal system usually takes place between 11p.m. and 1a.m. in the morning. The gallbladder uses the same time to release the toxin build up in the body. If you happen to be awake when both these functions are taking place within your body, there is the possibility of the toxin backing up to the liver which can endanger your health very badly. Sleeping late are byproducts of modern living styles. However, the human body was created in synchronization of nature and its activities. That is why before the advent of electricity people used to go to bed just after sundown and wake up with sunrise.

2. Don't alter your bedtimes haphazardly. Try to stick to a pattern where you go to bed and wake up at the same time. This should be done even on weekends. The continuous pattern will help your body to fit into a rhythm.

3. Maintain a soothing bedtime routine. This can change from person to person. You can use deep breathing exercises, meditation, use of aromatherapy, a gentle relaxing massage given by your partner, or even going through a complete and relaxing skin care routine. The secret is to get into a rhythm which makes you comfortable, relaxed, and ready for bed. Repeating it every day will help in easing out the tensions of the day.

4. Refrain from taking any heavy fluids two hours before bed time. This habit will minimize the number of times you need to visit the bathroom in the middle of the night. You should also make a habit of going to the bathroom just before you get into bed, so that you will not get the urge during night time.

5. Eat a meal enriched with proteins several hours before your bed time. The protein will enhance the production of L-tryptophan which is essential for the production of serotonin and melatonin. Follow up your meal with some fruit to help the tryptophan to cross easily across the blood brain barrier.

6. Refrain from taking any snacks while in bed or just before bed and reduce the level of sugar and grains in your dinner time as it will raise the blood sugar level, delaying sleep. When the body starts metabolizing these elements and the blood sugar level start dropping you will find yourself suddenly awake and unable to go back to sleep.

7. A hot bath before bed is found to be very soothing. When the body temperature is stimulated to a raised level during late evening by the time you get into bed, it will be ready to drop, signaling slumber time to your brain.

8. Stop your work and put them away ideally one to two hours before bed. The interval between work and bedtime should be used for unwinding from the pressure and tension of work. It is essential that you approach your bed with a calm mind instead of being hyped up about some matter.

9. If you prefer reading, a novel with an uplifting story instead of a stimulating one like suspense or mystery is recommended. Or the suspense will keep you up half the night awake trying to visualize

the end to the mystery!

A Few Lifestyle Suggestions to Make You Sleep Better

Don't take medications and drugs unless it is absolutely necessary for your health and wellbeing. A majority of prescribed and over the counter drugs can cause changes in your sleeping patterns.

Avoid drinks with alcohol or caffeine. Caffeine takes longer to metabolize in the body so that your body will experience its effects much longer after consumption. That is why even the cup of coffee you had in the evening will keep you awake during the night. Some of the medications and drugs in the market also contain caffeine which account for their capacity to generate sleeping irregularities. Though alcohol can make you feel drowsy the effect is very much short lived. Once the feeling goes away, you will find that sleep is eluding you for many hours and even the sleep that you finally reach will not take you to deep slumber after alcohol. In the absence of deep sleep, your body will not be able to perform its usual healing and regeneration process is vital for lasting healthiness.

Engage in regular exercise activities. If you are contained in an 8-hour office job, you should make sure that your body receives plenty of exercise which can dramatically increase your sleep health. The best time to exercise is, however, not closer to your bedtime but in the morning.

Keep away from sensitive food types that will keep you awake at night like sugar, pasteurized dairy foods, and grains. These foods can result in congestion, leading to gastric disorders.

The sleep apnea risk is enhanced amongst people with weight issues. If you think you have gained a few extra pounds and during this time you have also experienced sleeping trouble focus on losing the extra weight as a priority. The sleeping issue will correct automatically.

If your body is going through a hormone upheaval like during menopausal or premenopausal time, seek advice from your family physician, as this time can lead to sleeping difficulties.

Want to read more? Purchase our book on **Effective Guide On How to Sleep Well Everyday** *today!*

www.ingramcontent.com/pod-product-compliance
Lightning Source LLC
Chambersburg PA
CBHW030617220526
45463CB00004B/1329